From 100 to 0 in 1 Second

Preface

Joachim (Jim) Stark lives with his wife Sylvia and his three adult sons since 2001 in the USA. He was the General Manager in his brothers company from 2002 until February 2013.

The last of more than 10 accidents on 09/29/2012 left him with 7 broken ribs, a punctured lung and brain injury and did change his life drastically.

Resulting this major accident, Jim had lots of time to speak with God. His until then eventful life made him write this biography.

The title "from 100 to 0 in 1 second" is mirroring his life story.

Acknowledgment

Thanks to my wife, Sylvia

E-mail from March 16, 2015

Hi, Sweetheart,

Just finished the corrections on the book. At the same time, I came back to the conclusion that this book must be made accessible to people. As so often said: If God wants a book to be published, He will make it happen - in His time.

All the e-mails that you sent to the people who prayed for me after the accident should be included in the book, so they are in the Epilogue. I read the emails again.

Everything that happened at that time-and probably the three or four months after the last accident- is lost to my memory. When I read your e-mails, I was again aware of what you had to go through on the one hand, and on the other, all the things you did for me.

When we made our marriage vows almost thirty-four years ago, we promised each other that we would stay together in "good times as well as in bad times." You kept your promise - what you did for me after the accident was almost superhuman. You have stood behind me like a rock and have never given up. Surely, it was very often exasperating, especially with my 100% memory loss at the time, but you did not show it - at least not on the outside and not to me.

It was certainly a very difficult and hard time for you, but the Lord led you through it. I would, therefore, like to thank you wholeheartedly with all that I am and have, and thank and thank and thank you. I also thank God that He has placed such a great, awesome woman in my life. He already knew from the beginning what kind of woman I needed, and He gave me exactly what I needed.

I love you so much. Jim

iii

Table of Contents

v

1 Childhood

"Dad - look, the dredge over there! When I grow up, I'll be an excavator!"

"Daddy, why does the light flash next to the steering wheel?"

"Papa, Markus said..." and on went my chatter.

"Dad - look, the bike is so bent and it doesn't turn around at all!"

I must have been quite chatty as a four-year-old, and that's exactly what Papa needed. That should have helped him to not fall asleep while driving, despite his fatigue. My father got up at four in the morning. Thanks to the big family and the thriving business, my father and mother always had a lot to be done.

Father had to stop laying tiles a long time ago. As an entrepreneur with several employees, he not only managed the company, but also supervised the work on the construction sites. The tiles had to be laid in a timely manner and also perfectly installed; and of course, just as the customers wanted.

This era of life was good for me as well, because on the construction site trips I had my daddy for me alone and did not have to fight the competition of my then five siblings. On the construction site, I always felt a bit bigger than usual when walking with my father, for he was the Boss. In addition, it was a great feeling to sit in the front seat of the car, even if I could hardly look out of the window. And I recall another thing: Papa always had sweets for me!

* * *

One day we were on the road again visiting construction sites. Apparently, I was not as chatty that day, and my father fell asleep at the wheel. At the next corner, the car left the road and rushed down a steep hill. There were no safety belts at the time, so I flew through the windshield, out of the car. After the car flipped, the car landed right next to me on the grass. Just a few inches more, and my life would have come to an end! My father was bleeding on his forehead, and I had a broken leg.

Even though I was so young, I can still precisely remember two things about the accident. First: Father slowly closed his eyes while driving and he fell asleep. Why I did not wake him up is still a mystery to me. Second: I recall lying in the hospital, always on my back, with the right leg in the extension bandage where I could not move. Back then patients were confined to bed for six weeks. Imagine how hard it is for an active 4-year-old to lay still for six weeks!

* * *

Visiting construction sites ended when I started school. The elementary school was in our little village, and the school held all four classes in one room. There were only forty children in our elementary school. There was only one teacher who had to teach each class individually. Nevertheless, he somehow knew how to teach all the classes the appropriate material for each age group. Hats off to our teacher!

After the fourth grade, I went to the middle school or Hauptschule in a village four kilometers away for the next five years. My only challenge was to be on the bus early in the morning. Classes were scheduled only in the morning. After school and after my homework was done, I played with my friends in the woods or sometimes in or around the village of Wimmental. That is, if I was allowed! Everything was growing - not just my body, but also the family and the company. Very often, I couldn't play with my friends since I had to help in the company, which I did not like at all - construction site visits with my father were much more enjoyable! On some days I had to work as soon as the homework was done, and sometimes I worked even before homework was done, leaving me to do my studies after dinner.

During the school breaks, I often had to help my older brother, Werner (he was a tile-setter) on his jobsites. I brought him the materials, mixed mortar, grouted, and cleaned the tools in the evening. And much more.

Once, we had a larger construction site, which was a high-rise with 15 floors and three apartments per floor. The tiles had to be carried up the stairs by hand, including the mortar and the material for the grouting. That was my job all day long. For each apartment, there were 15 boxes of tiles, that's 45 boxes per floor, plus mortar and grout. Because I took over the transport of the materials and tile, my brother could concentrate on laying tiles - so he was very effective - and that helped the company.

The business continued to grow, and there was always something new to build. At first, the office was in the house. My family then added an office building with a small warehouse. The company outgrew the building, so we built a large warehouse, extended the office and set up a tile showroom. In order to deliver the material to the construction sites, a truck was purchased. It had to be loaded, so a forklift was added.

* * *

By the time I was perhaps twelve or thirteen, and the forklift was more or less my toy. I learned very quickly to drive and use it: tiles from our suppliers on palettes had to be unloaded and stored in our warehouse shelves and our truck had to be loaded in order to deliver the materials to our jobsites.

The forklift also served as a shovel loader - instead of the fork, a huge oval shovel was mounted. We could load up sand for mortar on our truck and deliver it to our jobsite, or use it in our small village to sell sand and deliver it with the forklift. Local customers needed sand in order to concrete their driveways or complete other projects on their property. As a 13-year-old, I often delivered sand and cement to our local customers, and I liked that a lot.

In Wimmental, there lived a man whose legs had both been amputated. One day, with my delivery, I drove past this man's house. His house was in a left-hand curve on the left-hand side of the road. Often when the weather was fine, I saw the man sitting in front of his house. I had been there many times and so it was not really interesting. But I had nothing better to do that day than to look at him closely, and was not paying attention to my driving when the right front wheel of the forklift caught the curb.

The forklift had three wheels, and when it caught the

curb, the whole thing tilted! It was a miracle that I was not buried under the forklift, which could have resulted in serious or even fatal injuries. The man sitting in front of his house had seen the accident and was totally shocked, but he could not help since his legs had been amputated, so I ran home immediately to get help.

My family resolved the minor accident without involving the police. That was really good for me, for 13-year-olds were usually not allowed to drive a forklift nor any other vehicles!

2 Our Extended Family

With seven children, the Stark Family was always busy. Add to this the rapid growth of our company, which demanded full attention and one hundred percent commitment. When a company grows, it constantly needs new employees. Since each human being is different in God's creation, there are always new challenges and problems.

The circumstances demanded discipline, and we learned that my father's word was law, and his position was always the right one. We were not allowed to even get the idea of discussing anything with him! Therefore, our education was very strict and with little expression of love from my father. I was (and presumably my siblings, too) very happy if we did not see our father all day long, yet we knew he loved us. I think his behavior as a father was very much connected with his own youth and how his parents had raised him.

My father had to go to war at the age of seventeen, to the Eastern Front in Russia where the situation was the worst. During battle, he was seriously injured in the left leg by a gunshot wound. Like all the wounded, my father was taken to the hospital where he remained for several months until he was fully recovered. To this day, my father has never told us any details about his war experiences on the front line. I am certain it was a life-changing experience for a 17-year-old, and I am also certain that he was strongly influenced by the war.

My father's father was a very strict man. I didn't know my grandfather. He died before I came into the world. I did have a chance to get to know my father's mother. She was always a loving, sweet, and tender personality. I liked to visit her, often accompanied by my mother, and Grandma always had something sweet to offer me. Even without the treats, I looked forward to visiting her at any time.

Although Grandma could hardly walk because of her severe arthritis and suffered great pain, she was always happy and saw the good in everything. When we visited her, she spoke a lot about God and also said that she would pray a lot, especially for her seven grandchildren and our parents. She was very hard of hearing. She sometimes did not notice that we were entering the apartment, and I could hear her quietly praying. I know that Grandma really prayed a lot. I am sure that she prayed for us for many hours every day in the last years of her life! Back then, I did not think much about it, but today I know that my grandmother and her many prayers, especially her divine relationship with God, have played a very important role in the further spiritual development of our family.

* * *

My parents were very religious. For the whole family, it was the rule to go to church every Sunday and Thursday night. In the beginning, I was bored during church services and I endured it with difficulty. When I was old enough, I became an altar boy, which was part of our tradition in the village. My brothers were also altar boys and probably almost all of the boys in the village served as altar boys.

I was not as bored with the services when I became an altar boy. I liked to ring the bell, enter the church in procession with the priest, and to hold a candle at the bible readings. As an altar boy, I also felt a bit important! In addition, altar boys sat next to the priest so that we could see all the people from the front, and not just the few heads in the row in front of us. I was not certain at the time what spiritual function a bell ringer served and what the whole thing had to do with God. I don't remember anyone explaining that to me. It was just a part of the village life and any small change alleviated the boredom of going two times a week to church.

There was even more to our Sundays: After lunch we walked 15 minutes up a little hill to a small chapel where we had to pray the Rosary. Every Sunday! This did not suit me at all, because my friends did not have to pray the Rosary. My friends had fun doing whatever they wanted to do on Sunday afternoons and I had to pray the Rosary! At the time, I did not appreciate the beautiful, awesome view over the whole town from the chapel on the hilltop.

At some point my father took over the leadership of the Rosary prayer, and from then on I had to be there every Sunday a few minutes earlier to unlock the door and light the candles at the little altar. In addition to my family, a handful of people came and prayed for about half an hour. I thought these Sunday afternoon Rosaries were very boring and unpleasant at the time.

At home, too, we prayed a lot: each morning, before each lunch, and before we went to bed another five to ten minutes was required for the evening prayer. There were always the same sentences that we, well, "reeled off", without thinking about what we prayed and without knowing really the purpose of it. On Sundays, the evening prayer lasted almost half an hour, which was particularly annoying to me because we were required to pray standing up. My father made sure that everybody attended.

* * *

My father could make life very uncomfortable for us, and I shall only share a few examples: At lunch, my younger sister always sat to the right of my father. At the slightest mistake, she earned a loud exhortation or sometimes even a slap. Times were especially tense when there were difficulties in the company, when employees were not working properly, or when angry customers had complained. All the anger, which had dammed up in my father, was vented on us at the smallest occasion. Everyone who had done something wrong was beaten. Most of the time, we could already see on his face what would happen if we did something wrong. So we made a point to be especially quiet in order not to upset him. If, on the other hand, everything was going well in the company and my father was relaxed and happy, then life was good at my father's table at lunch.

My mother was the good soul of the family, a loving and calm person who always strove to create peace and mediate between father and children. She always stood by our side, which sometimes brought my father's loud attack upon her. I still admire my mother today as she endured it without fighting back or attacking my father. However, she often had tears in her eyes.

As we grew older, we children gradually took over responsibility in the company, and in the process, my father changed for the good. My father and I grew to have a super relationship as a son can only wish for.

Because of his severity, honesty, justice and straightforwardness, he imparted hard words upon his children, but overall his criticism was correct. My father was very respectful of employees, suppliers and others in the whole industry.

One of my brothers, as also my father, was named Richard. My brother, Richard was born paralyzed. I cannot remember that my father ever gave him a harsh word or shouted at him. Father always treated Richard with respect and love, which was something special for me. I am really proud of my father for that!

My father's behavior was influenced by having five sons, of which one was physically disabled, and two daughters, plus a growing company and an excess of work with much stress and too little sleep. Today, I cannot imagine how he coped with all of this: to raise seven children, to be head of a household and to have a growing business.

I also have special respect for my mother. She was a wife, mother of seven children, and the boss of a growing business. Every morning and every evening she had to care for my paralyzed brother, Richard. She carried him down the stairs to put him on the ground floor in the wheelchair. This became increasingly difficult with Richard's age and weight. Nevertheless, she did it because he was her child and she loved him. Although she had to work really hard, I never heard her complaining.

3 My "Angel on Earth"

My brother, Richard was four years older than I was, and we were very close. In my childhood he was like an "angel on earth" who accompanied me; Americans would say he was my best "buddy". Whenever I had time, as a small boy, I went on outings with him. We were a well-established team: I pushed him in his wheelchair and Richard steered.

We loved to be outdoors in nature and often roamed the most impossible places in our village of Wimmental. Little hills, pastures, vineyards and forests surround Wimmental. The wheelchair was without an electric motor, of course - and the brakes were primitive, so I needed a lot of power to move my brother. Sometimes my brother needed a lot of courage to handle what I did to wheel him around.

I recall one event in which we were once again traveling too fast. "Race-driver Biberle" bounced along a dirt road, and when the front wheel struck a stone, the whole chair, together with the passenger, tipped forward. Richard flew from the wheelchair to the ground and the wheelchair flew behind him, right on him! As he was paralyzed from the waist down, he could do nothing. As an eight-year-old, I was too small and not strong enough to prevent the fall.

I still do not know how we both managed to get him back into the wheelchair - Richard was twelve or thirteen at the time and weighed about 110 pounds. Somehow we managed to do it by combining forces. Except for a few bruises, my brother had no serious injuries.

Even with that, it was not the end of our adventures together! No matter what we did, even when I hurt him in my childish carelessness, he never complained or reproached me. As I said, he was just my "angel on earth".

* * *

Because of his disability, Richard could not go to school, so a teacher came to the house. And, of course, Richard had to do homework. Nevertheless, he always had a lot of time, so he read a lot of books and thereby acquired enormous knowledge.

Richard and I shared a room. In the evening before we fell asleep, we talked for a long time. Richard had so much to tell, and it was often interesting to hear what he had read. Sometimes he told me exciting stories from his books - so we had great times both night and day!

Just as my mother was always anxious to maintain or restore peace, Richard was a real peacemaker. I can't remember any single time that he raised his voice. He was the peace-boy in the family.

* * *

When I got home from school, I always went to our room first to talk to Richard and tell him what was new at school. One day a shock awaited me: Richard was in his bed half-erect as I had never before seen him, and he was foaming at the mouth. My mother was with him, and she was crying. I realized that something bad was happening to my brother! I immediately turned around and began to cry too when suddenly my nose started bleeding from the shock! What was wrong with my brother, my buddy? Just moments later, the paramedics came up the stairs and took him on a stretcher to the ambulance. Richard was rushed to the hospital in Heilbronn.

We visited Richard the next day at the hospital, and the doctors said it was critical. Richard had always had an open wound on his back, which was the source of his paralysis. Because of the wound in his back, a serious infection had poisoned his brain, leading to the attack. Richard was in danger of another attack at any time, so he had to be kept on a strict diet from that day forward.

My brother lived with so many restrictions anyway, but he had always enjoyed good food. Now he could no longer eat all the good things he had liked so much. At least Richard was allowed to leave the hospital after only a few days, and soon we returned to our routine together.

Although he was required to stick to a strict diet, I never heard Richard whine nor complain. He was grateful for all that our mother did for him. She cooked a special diet for him - and he appreciated it very much.

However, the attack left its mark. He was no longer the old Richard, as I had known him! I think he knew that his time with us would come to an end. It came, as the doctors had said. After only two months, Richard had another attack and he was admitted to the hospital. This time the doctors could no longer help, and he died in peace a few days later.

Many people came to his funeral. Richard had not gone to school, yet through the company, many people had gotten to know him as a lovable person. So with a heavy

13

heart and many tears I said goodbye to my "angel on earth".

4   Youth

After middle school, or the Hauptschule, my parents decided to send me to the Wirtschaftsschule or economic & commercial school for two years in Stuttgart. My accommodations were in Kolpingheim boarding house, where only young men between the ages of 14 and 23 lived. Most of them attended a secondary school or got specific job training, which was not possible in their hometowns. At the age of 14, I was one of the youngest students in Kolpingheim.

I went to school by streetcar every day. The stop was only three minutes away from Kolpinghiem. As a rule, after school let out on Friday, I went every other weekend by train to Heilbronn where I was picked up by relatives who were nearby, or I took the bus for the twelve kilometers to Wimmental. I returned to Stuttgart on Sunday evening the same way.

My two years at Stuttgart gave me a very important experience: I was introduced to alcohol and learned how alcohol combined with nicotine along with only three hours of sleep at night affected the body and mind. I quickly learned to be consistent and to say no, even if it was not easy and the temptation was great. I also had to learn to associate with the right people. I learned that decisions led to either good or bad consequences, so it is important to make the right decisions.

During this time, I became a fan of the VfB Stuttgart, which had risen from the second soccer league to the first league. Soccer had always interested me and for two or three years, I played in the B and A youth team in a neighboring town's soccer club. In Stuttgart, a friend and classmate of mine was a longtime VfB Stuttgart fan. Klaus had a season ticket for the A-Block in the stadium (which is still the main Fan Block of the Stuttgart VfB) and gave me access to the Fan Block, which was a small miracle. I was able to see how true fans were fanatically two hundred percent behind their team, no matter what happened. Even if "they" lost the game, the fans stood like a wall behind their team. During a game I knew better than to say any negative word about the VfB; otherwise, I would have gotten a beating!

I had learned a lesson for life, for later I became a fan in a very different "league"- in His league, and I know with whom I am standing - "in good times as well as in bad times".

* * *

While living in Stuttgart, I had a bumpy encounter, which luckily went off without injury. One day after school, I went with my friends to the streetcar station, and we were talking splendidly. I was probably very tired, as I often was in those years. I had to cross the tracks, so I said goodbye to my friends - and did not notice that there was a streetcar coming! I ran into the streetcar -- or perhaps the streetcar hit me with the right front! Thank God I was thrown away from the car and didn't get caught underneath the wheel. It was close! Many people hurried in and offered help, asking if everything was okay and whether I had any injuries. In spite of the strong impact, I had only a few scrapes. It was unbelievable that I was safe, yet it was true.

After finishing school in Stuttgart, I began my training as a wholesale salesman in a Heilbronn company. The company was considerably larger than my parents' company. There were several departments, among them a tile department. It was not totally new territory for me. In the larger company, I was able to use everything I had learned at my parents' company.

I did not like that I had to take the bus to work. I enrolled in driving school and I made it my big goal to get my drivers license at exactly the age of 18! Indeed, I passed the driving test and picked up my driver's license on my birthday at the Landratsamt or courthouse.

Of course, I also made sure that I had a car when I turned 18. I bought an Alfa Romeo from my older brother and paid for it from my own income. Like my siblings, I also received a small subsidy from my father for the first car, but the rest I had to earn through my job. Since I had already worked regularly as a child and earned a little money, it was no problem to pay cash for the car plus tax and insurance.

* * *

Before my 18th birthday, I often went with my friend, Bernd to places in in Wimmental, where he also lived. Bernd was six weeks older than me and received his driver's license a few weeks before me. He was motivated to have a car because he wanted to visit his girlfriend, Bettina in Stuttgart. Bernd enjoyed the 43-mile drive to Stuttgart. Since I knew and liked Stuttgart for its flair, I went with him and met his girlfriend, Bettina.

Two weeks before my 18th birthday, I went back to Stuttgart with Bernd. Bettina suggested we all visit a discotheque in downtown and she invited her friend, Sylvia to come along. Said and done! Bernd, of course, spent his time with Bettina, for they danced a lot together. So it was clear that I was to take care of Sylvia.

I had never had a proper relationship with a girl and was, therefore, a bit shy. I was very impressed with Sylvia at first sight. Everything about her: clothes, hair, hands, body, what she said and how she said it, all this immediately touched me. Somehow we had long conversations despite my shyness - and we understood each other very well. At the end of the evening, we arranged to meet again the next weekend!

The following weekend, I was allowed to ride with Bernd and we visited the same discotheque. That night, we kissed for the first time and afterwards it was clear: Sylvia was my first girlfriend! The next weekend, I already had a car and driver's license, and was no longer dependent on my friend's service. After our third date, I was completely in love with Sylvia and could think of nothing else but her. The deeper the relationship became, the more often we met during the week, in spite of the three-hour drive between us.

* * *

The time came to introduce myself to Sylvia's parents. One Saturday, we went back to a discotheque, this time to Ludwigsburg, approximately 9 miles away from Stuttgart. I wanted the opportunity to meet Sylvia's parents the next day. When we were leaving the discotheque, four people were looking for a ride to Stuttgart. My Alfa Romeo had only five seats, so Sylvia and another girl sat in the passenger seat. The other three people sat in the back seat and we left Ludwigsburg overloaded.

18

I always drove in the fast lane, probably because I wanted to impress my new girlfriend and her friends, and show them how well I mastered my car. Since I had driven fork-lifts, trucks and other company vehicles adeptly from a young age, I was confident that I had my new car completely under control from the get go. At least that's what I thought.

It had rained and the road was wet. I drove along the river Neckar at high speed for miles, and it turned sharply to the left towards the Neckar Bridge. My full braking proved to be a big mistake: the front wheels locked and we slid towards the river. The guardrail gave way, but offered enough resistance that the car came to a halt in the last second! Otherwise, we would all have fallen into the river!

By a miracle, the guardrail had not pushed through the windshield into the passenger compartment, which would have had serious consequences for my passengers. The force of the impact hurled Sylvia into the footwell, so she had bruises on both legs. Otherwise no one was hurt. The car, however, was so badly damaged that it was later declared a total loss by the insurance company. The towing service took my Alfa Romeo and me to Wimmental while the police drove Sylvia home.

The next day, I borrowed my mother's car to drive to Stuttgart to meet Sylvia's family as we had planned. It was the first of April which is April Fools Day, but for me it was not funny at all. I was not anxious to talk to Sylvia's father and to report what had happened the night before. I could imagine what Sylvia's parents must have thought when their daughter was brought home late at night by the police!

The weekend was unforgettable for all involved.

5   A Miracle in Itself

It's still a mystery to me, what impressed Sylvia about me. Maybe it was our first accident together? In any case, we were inseparable from the beginning. After the Alfa Romeo, I bought an Audi. My visits to Stuttgart became even more frequent. Especially on weekends, we were always up very late, because we could not separate. Often I went home in the middle of the night, not wanting to leave her.

It was late summer, and we had known each other for almost six months. One Sunday night, I was on the highway on the way home to Wimmental. Completely exhausted, I fell asleep while in a long drawn left curve, and once again the guardrail proved to be a life guard: I slid along the guardrail until I awoke; fortunately, the car did not sideslip. The damages on the right side of the vehicle were significant, but my comprehensive insurance took over the high costs of the repair in full.

A few months later, I went home from the business school in Heilbronn.

In my education to become a certified businessman, I usually had 2 weeks school and 4 weeks practical training or internship in the company as part of my education. My business school was located close to downtown. One day on my way back home, I left business school, drove through downtown Heilbronn and passed through the city center. I saw a car at a small crossroads to my right. Since I was on the main road, I had the right of way and drove straight ahead without reducing my speed. The driver of the other car must have completely overlooked me and drove into the intersection. Everything happened so fast! I couldn't brake in time and crashed head-on into the left fender of the other vehicle.

At that time, there was no law to wear a seat belt while driving and I enjoyed the luxury or the freedom not to "click it". However, in that situation, it was not a good idea. So I bounced and my forehead hit the windshield, which obviously was not created for such a load. The glass cut my forehead open and the chips splashed into my skull. Of course, my forehead started bleeding like crazy, and how! The lady who caused the accident ran from her car to mine and was totally shocked when she saw me. My bloody face and skull shocked her. She apologized a hundred times.

Within minutes, the police were there, along with the rescue vehicle. I was taken to the hospital, where I was examined from head to foot for further injuries. Luckily, there was nothing else to find. The nurse informed me that my forehead had to be sewn, and that the doctor would come in a minute. They did not give me any painkillers. I sat alone for a long half an hour with a lot of pain and no doctor. I thought perhaps they'd forgotten me?

When they rediscovered me, they had to first clean up the pool of blood that had formed on the floor below me. Before the doctor could sew the wound, he had to remove all of the small glass chips from the wound. Still without painkillers! The doctor ran his finger over the wound, and when he spotted a splinter, he removed it with the tweezers. This process took a long time because the glass splinters were very small and in fine fragments. The doctor wanted to be sure that there was no glass left in the wound before sewing me up with many stitches.

I was still without pain treatment! Perhaps the doctor thought somebody had already given me something against the pain? I don't know, but in today's world, some forty years later, the doctor might have a huge lawsuit against him.

Sylvia could only visit me once in the hospital. She was 16 years old and didn't drive yet. That hurt me the most; I would have liked to have her with me at this time. On her one and only visit, she barely recognized me: the entire forehead was considerably swollen, and my face was quite bulky.

While in the hospital, I had the time to think about life and death. For the first time, I realized that God protected me every day. My parents and grandparents prayed every day for His protection. I cannot imagine how many accidents I would have had because of my fast life and driving style. I thank God for his protection!

My car was declared a total loss; the other car had only minor body damage. I was overjoyed and surprised that my insurance company took over all costs without discussion, and even paid me for the pain and suffering. With this money, I bought an Alfa Romeo again.

* * *

It was late autumn. On a late departure from Stuttgart, it began to snow heavily, and my car still had summer tires on it. I could have stayed at Sylvia's place. Heilbronn is at lower elevation (659 feet) than Stuttgart (804 feet), so I thought it had probably rained and not snowed on the highway to Heilbronn. The road conditions, however, proved just the opposite: the closer I got to Heilbronn, the more snow lay on the road.

About halfway home, on a downhill slope, I saw the all the cars a few hundred yards ahead of me slowing to a standstill. With my summer tires, a full braking would not have been helpful, and I presumed the car would only have slipped. So I tried to slow down with stutter brakes; unfortunately, it did not reduce my speed very much. I decided to change to the emergency lane on the right side in order to avoid a collision with the other cars ahead of me, but did not succeed due to my summer tires and the snowy road. I crashed into the car in front of me. This time I had the seat belt on – I had learned my lesson from the glass chips in my forehead from the previous accident - so I did not have any injuries, despite the strong impact. Fortunately, the other driver also remained uninjured. Sadly, another new car was a total loss...

Today, I am the father of adult sons, and I have often been in the same position as my parents and my in-laws. How did they cope with all my accidents? The fact that Sylvia's parents still had the confidence to let their daughter ride with me was a miracle.

* * *

The relationship between Sylvia and me was very intense after a short time: Sylvia was supposed to be my wife! She was sixteen when I first asked for her hand in marriage. Unfortunately, it was not the right time to marry because she was still a trainee in Stuttgart, and I was about to graduate. We decided to wait on marriage until Sylvia had finished her education.

It is an advantage if you have older brothers! I had never doubted that. Having older brothers saved me from the 15 months of becoming a soldier, so I returned to my parents' company after my final examination. On re-entering our company, I tried practical work as a concrete layer. At that time our company had expanded continuously to four departments (tiles, concreting, flooring, sales). Before long, we all realized that my talents were more in business where I was educated and not in the craft.

At 62 years of age, my father decided to place the responsibility for the company in younger hands. The management was transferred to my oldest brother, Werner. My oldest sister, Regina was responsible for payroll. Another brother was a skilled floor installer, who took over the management of the sales and flooring department.

I have great respect for my father that he knew the right time to pass the scepter and the entire responsibility from his hand to the next generation. My father became involved primarily in the sales department, where he was able to contribute more than forty years of professional experience for the benefit of customers. They greatly appreciated his excellent advice, which he enjoyed a lot.

After my father had given the responsibility for the company to my brother, he changed for the better, for he was so free, happy, and easy- going. The whole family enjoyed the really super-good father we had always wanted.

I began as a clerk for the tile and concrete department at my parents' company after completing business school. That brought me in contact with all kinds of people, customers, employees, suppliers and banks. I more or less grew up with the company from a young age, and was already familiar with a lot of procedures, so I learned quickly.

* * *

Two months before Sylvia's 19th birthday, she successfully completed her education as a bank clerk. I had a good job, so nothing was in the way for our marriage. We were both very young. She was still 18 and I had celebrated my 21st birthday a few weeks earlier.

One of my dreams was to spend our honeymoon traveling on a motorcycle. So I decided to buy a visually beautiful and powerful 750-Kawasaki motorcycle. Sylvia's parents were totally against it. My father forbade me even to buy the machine, and my mother advised me against it almost every day in her loving way. Perhaps I wanted my father to see that he would no longer be the master of the house soon, so I bought the bike anyway.

A few days later, I received my first lesson on the motorcycle. To get to the next town, you had to turn to the right from our house, and after a long straight sharp right into the roundabout. It was a nice warm day, so after work I went for a spin. As always, I started with super acceleration - from 0 to 100 in 4.5 seconds!

At the last minute in the roundabout, I saw a car coming from the left and braked at full strength. Unfortunately, I only engaged the brake on the front wheel. I was already slightly out of line with the roundabout, so the front wheel lost contact with the ground. The motorcycle tilted to the right side with me still on it and we skittered in the direction of the oncoming vehicle.

In a flash, I could see myself already buried under the car, but thanks to the quick reaction of the driver - and by God's intervention - the car pulled to the opposite side of the street and onto the shoulder of the road. Luckily, we were alone on the road, so a collision at the last minute was prevented. I received large abrasions all over my right leg and right arm that were extremely painful, but I had no other injuries, and the bike had only scratches.

Therefore, I could realize my dream to drive the motorcycle the day after the wedding for our honeymoon. Actually, I drove the bike and Sylvia drove our car, so we could use either vehicle, depending on the weather conditions.

Our honeymoon lodging was a vacation apartment in Bavaria at the foothills of the Alps. In good weather we toured the German and Austrian Alps by motorcycle, and we took the car when it rained. It was an amazing place for our honeymoon. Everything went fine and we enjoyed the wonderful trips by bike. Unfortunately, this beautiful time on the motorcycle was over too soon.

6 From 100 to 0 in 1 Second, Part One

At the beginning of our marriage, we rented a studio in my sister's house in Wimmental. We got comfortable with the little studio, with our new life, our new schedule, and with ourselves. My wife started working at the same bank where she had received her training because they had a branch in Heilbronn. Six weeks after our wedding, I wanted to meet with Sylvia at noon for lunch in Heilbronn. The weather was fine, so naturally I took the Kawasaki.

I was traveling on the main road to the next village, when on the right I saw a car that wanted to turn into the main road. Because I was sure that the motorist had seen me, I continued on at full speed.

Unfortunately, I was wrong; the vehicle turned into the main street and caught me on the right leg. The force of the impact catapulted me against the old schoolhouse next to the road. I slid with the bike and my shoulder along the schoolhouse wall and then I was thrown into the street. The motorcycle crashed diagonally across a wall.

My head was clear at first and in the first few seconds I felt okay. I realized I was just lying in the middle of the road, and that was not okay. I wanted to get up and get off the road in order to avoid being run over from oncoming cars! Then I noticed that there was not much left of my leg - and pain set in as I had never experienced before.

After a few minutes the ambulance and the paramedics came. A passerby probably called them. My father, who had received the news from our company radio, arrived at the scene at about the same time as the ambulance. I can still recall my dad's tears and despair when he saw my leg. Even more, it devastated my father when I told the paramedics that I had no feeling in my whole body, except for the intense pain. My father's despair was understandable, for he had immediately thought of my brother, Richard and he was worried that my injuries could also result in paraplegia. It turned out later that my numbness was caused by shock.

* * *

With blue lights and sirens, they carried me to the nearest Hospital where they found a comminuted fracture to my right lower leg and a fracture to my left shoulder. Thankfully, I had no injuries to the spine. That was a relief! The doctors later told me they had debated at great length on how they should treat the lower leg, and whether they should amputate it because the bone was totally smashed. My doctors finally decided to save my leg and to create a kind of metal scaffolding to keep the lower leg together, which also granted them continual access to the wound. Similar to my first accident at the age of four, I was not allowed to leave my bed.

The first two or three days in the hospital were quite good. The strong painkillers given me by the paramedics at the scene of the accident and continued by my doctors did an excellent job. I had no pain and felt pretty good. However, after two or three more days, the extreme pain returned and my mind became clear again. I thought about the accident and the position in which I found

29

myself. I was bedridden. I thought perhaps I would lose my leg. No one could tell me when I could get out of bed and get out of the hospital. I was newly married. My wife, whom I loved very much, was home alone after just six weeks of marriage. I did not know if I could ever walk again properly, or even play sports, and, and, and ... such thoughts were my constant companions.

Sylvia visited me every day, as did the whole family and my friends who came to see me regularly. On one visit my younger sister asked if she could see the wound on my lower leg. A cloth covered my wound. I asked her several times if she really wanted to see it. She remained resolute, so I pulled back the cloth. When she saw my leg with the open wound without dressing, she passed out.

* * *

After two weeks in the hospital, the doctors couldn't give me any positive news. At this time I was so mentally down that I announced to my wife that I probably would not get out of the hospital alive.

In one second, "from one hundred to zero": My bike needed to accelerate from zero to a hundred in four and a half seconds, but the accident happened in only one second! Until then, everything was wonderful: I was newly married, full of love, zest and joy, full of plans for the future - and within one second, everything was different. I was at zero.

Isn't it interesting: Most of us only think about life and the purpose of life when we reach the bottom. For me it was no different. In my time at the hospital, I contemplated my church visits, the Rosary prayers, and especially my relationship with God.

For me, there was no question that God exists. With so many prayers while growing up in my parents' house, I knew how to pray. Only the question remained in my mind - whether God heard the prayers of such a young and unimportant guy like me? There were not many alternatives, so I said this prayer:

"Dear God, I know that You exist. You see my hopeless situation. Please, please, help me and open up a way that I can leave the hospital in five weeks! I want to be with my wife, whom I love so much and miss. Thank You, God, for taking care of everything. Amen."

A few minutes after the prayer all my "I do not want to live" thoughts were gone. A confidence came into my heart that all would be well again.

The next day the doctor came to me and told me, after a lot of thinking and investigating, that he had decided to operate on me. He wanted to replace the missing bone parts by taking bone out from my pelvic region. It was not going to be a simple procedure, yet he was confident that all would go well. There would probably still be some small bone pieces missing, but those gaps in my leg would fill in by themselves. If everything went well, I could leave the hospital in a month.

I was overjoyed at the good news - and it arrived the day after my simple prayer to God. Moreover, I was allowed to leave the hospital 3 weeks earlier than originally anticipated. Overall, I had "only" six and a half weeks' hospital stay; and that was a miracle considering the injury.

As a young married couple, the experience confirmed to us that God exists and that He hears and answers our prayers, if it fits into His plan for us. From that day forward, Sylvia and I prayed together several times a week, and we prayed as I had learned from my parents.

7 Young Father, Young Boss

Once I was somewhat recovered, I was needed in the company, so I returned to work. I grew more and more into my job and took on more responsibility.

About that time, my oldest brother, Werner, our CEO, received an offer to build a tile showroom in the United States for a German-American company. This had always been his dream, so he did not want to miss the opportunity. He decided to leave for 6 weeks and breathe American air. He put me in charge before his departure, and flew across the pond.

The client was impressed by my brother and offered Werner a position as CEO in the company. What a deal! Without hesitation, Werner accepted. Werner had announced his decision by phone to us, so when he came back, the big question was: Who would take his post? We had at least 40 employees in four different departments! My other brother had no interest to become the big boss. My sister Regina and her husband rejected it also. My father didn't want to take over again. I was the only one left. At the age of 23, I became the new boss.

* * *

Sylvia was pregnant and before the birth of our first son, we moved into our own house. We built it according to our specifications and with a lot of personal contribution. I was present at the birth of our first son, but I had no idea what to expect. My wife was in severe pain, so I asked the midwife whether she had a painkiller. It was an unforgettable moment! Completely shocked, the midwife informed me that this was not severe pain but completely normal labor! So that issue was settled. After 13 hours in the delivery room, our first son Patrick came into the world and the new family was founded.

Soon after the birth of our first son, Sylvia was pregnant again. We decided that she would quit her job at the bank and work in our company in accounting. It allowed us flexibility in our schedules as the baby's needs required.

Once Werner moved to the U.S., his home (originally our parents' home) was empty. The house was situated next to the office and warehouse. After much deliberation, we sold the house we had built and loved so much, in order to move into our parents' former home. The move was advantageous for us, particularly for Sylvia and the baby. When our son, Patrick was sleeping, she could work for a few hours and readily take care of him when he awoke without having to commute between work and home.

* * *

For me, as the new boss, began a challenging life. The baby was indeed a new and wondrous experience. Not so wondrous was my job as boss. Many long-time employees were more than twice my age and many were in the age group of my father. Two employees had been with the company before I was born, and now this "youngster" was the boss! In the many power struggles that I faced, I became a tough, authoritarian businessman: I had to prove to everybody, including customers, suppliers, employees, especially the banks, and of course my family, that I was capable of leading and managing the company.

The responsibility and the constant pressure made me internally hard. The joyful, always good-humored boy was no longer there; instead, I became a tough businessman who enjoyed very little fun. I was up early and by five o'clock in the office, and I was the last to leave it. Working on Saturday was normal, and I spent at least a few hours on Sunday also. In time, the employees, the suppliers and the banks accepted me as boss. My urge to prove myself resulted in the company's revenue being doubled within a few years. My strength was that I made a personal appearance with clients, especially with large customers and for large orders. The management of key accounts were obviously impressed that I, the head of the company in my mid-twenties, appeared in person during the final negotiations.

Since I had grown up with the company, I knew every detail and could answer all of the questions in the negotiations to the complete satisfaction of the customer. Very often, customers decided to award the contract to me, sometimes committing to half a million DM (Deutsch Mark) or a quarter of a million dollars U.S.

* * *

Unfortunately, the mentality of a tough businessman also affected my behavior towards my wife. Like father, like son, I copied precisely the bad behavior of my father. Everything had to go my way and if it didn't, then I bellowed. The only difference between my father and I was how I dealt with my children. I told myself I would never raise my children as my father had raised me. My children were indeed raised very strict, but still brought up with love. They were super awesome and well-behaved children.

I recall one of our field trips with the local choir. I had joined the choir when I was 14-years-old and really enjoyed singing. Despite minor interruptions because of education or accidents, I was always "active" in the choir. That did not change after my marriage. I even took a conductor course and was appointed Second conductor. I had to conduct whenever the First Conductor had a conflict in his appointments. My wife was also a member of the choir, so it was natural for us to participate with the children in the annual field trip. When we accompanied our sons Patrick (age six) and Gilbert (age five) on the field trip, we were praised at the annual trip repeatedly for having such well-behaved children. We attended many other events as a family, and were praised for our 3 kids (our third child, Kevin arrived 7 years after Gilbert). Our kids have been always a joy and blessing for us. Although there were certainly unpleasant moments any parent experiences with kids in general, we cannot express how grateful we are to have them.

* * *

The company continued to develop and grow rapidly. To cope with the boost in sales, we sub-contracted out jobs in the tile department. Sub-contractors were only used as needed, when our own people had more jobs than they could handle. When we had less jobs, we employed our own people and not sub-contractors. Since sub-contractors were not hired or fired as regular employees, they did not cost extra money. This was an easy and inexpensive way to increase sales.

After the fall of the Berlin Wall and with the opening of the border to East Germany, we sensed a good opportunity to increase revenue again. Our tax consultants started branches right away in East Germany and asked us if we would be willing to take over a company in Delitzsch near Leipzig. It was a tile installation business, so for us it was not considered to be a new territory.

After much deliberation, many visits, and meetings on-site, we took over the company. My youngest brother, Markus, who had completed both a business education as well as having experience as a tile setter, declared himself ready to take on the "Adventure to the East ". Just married, he and his wife moved to East Germany and at first they lived in a small apartment on the premises.

I tried to support both activities and found myself at the branch in Delitzsch one or two days a week. I helped to implement the organization and procedures that had been proven successful in our main company.

The expansion turned out to be a really new field for us, and a great deal of work. None of the existing staff was accustomed to work efficiently, nor were they profit-oriented. They didn't know how to really work (not just talk or do nothing) for 9 hours a day. The older staff had an especially hard time to adapt new procedures, and wished the "old times" would come back. They had lived under the communist government, which told them what to do and how to do it, and actually trained them how not to work profitably. The younger employees, on the other hand, liked to adapt to new procedures and had no problem with all the changes we implemented. They saw that it all made sense and was a lot better. They quickly understood what was really important, and continued the innovations with enthusiasm, which was very motivating and encouraging for us.

Through contacts with our existing customers in the west, we were automatically in contact with their offices in the East. In a short time, we had more than enough jobs in East Germany. Almost all buildings had to be remodeled since the communist government had no money and could not invest anything to keep the buildings up-to-date.

It was a huge and heavy task, and Markus and his wife did an awesome job with turning everything around. In a short time, they formed a young and ambitious workforce, and once all the procedures had been handled and were clear, the business worked even better in East Germany than in our headquarters in West Germany!

Personally, I never had a chance to rest, for we were always moving forward. I wanted to show everyone what I was capable of. The next step was the establishment of a branch in Dresden with the same pattern as in Delitzsch. This time, we trained the future leaders for Dresden on the most important processes in our headquarters in West Germany. In a short amount of time, the Dresden branch was opened.

Then came the establishment of a branch in East Berlin. My sister, Regina and her husband agreed to manage the establishment of the branch.

All was excellent in Delitzsch, for my brother Markus handled this branch by himself. I could, therefore, limit my visits to Berlin and Dresden.

* * *

Ten years after I became the CEO of the Stark Company,

having been favored by the opening of the border to East Germany, our company with all its branches had 400 employees (including subcontractors), we achieved revenues of 40 million DM (approximately 20 million dollars U.S.) In business, I was extremely successful, but not as an individual: My relationship with my wife was getting worse. I developed more and more to being the dictator in my marriage and with my family.

Also, I was rarely at home because of my weekly visits to the branches in East Germany as well as the headquarters. My days consisted mostly of 14 to 15 hours of stress in its purest form – the work was not quite as I had imagined, for my main job was "a problem solver for all cases". My desk was full of problems! These daily burdens and responsibilities meant that by Sunday afternoon I would become restless and worried of all the tasks, problems and concerns that I knew would arise on Monday morning.

A kind of depression started within me each Sunday afternoon, and I was good for nothing. Not even my wife could help me. The children brought a little ray of light into the darkness, but even they could not change my total state of mind. My salary was very good, the car I drove was very fast and always had a special design, our family lifestyle was considered "high end", and yet all of this could not take the fear away. It seemed that nothing could bring back real joy into my life -- not even going to church on Sunday and praying the Rosary.

8 From Minus to Plus

During this time of darkness and stress, my sister, Regina put an invitation on my desk: "That might be something for you." It was an invitation to a three-day seminar on "Management with God". What was that all about, I wondered, and how can I manage the company with God? That was surely a joke!

A few days later, I looked at the invitation again and showed it to my wife. Back then, we very seldom agreed on anything. When Sylvia said that we should participate and pointed out the seminar didn't cost anything, I signed up for both of us.

The seminar took place in a beautiful hotel overlooking a lake in Switzerland. After we got settled into our room, we went to the meeting room. Of course, we did not know anyone and felt a bit uncomfortable, especially since we did not know what to expect. The manager introduced himself and talked about his life. He explained that he started the series of seminars "Management with God" after he discovered it really is possible to manage business, a personal life, and everything else with *God*.

In the very first lecture, he told us that "Management with God" does not refer primarily to the company, that it starts with our personal life first. We need God as a basis in our own lives, in our marriage and family; then we can make God also a basis in the company and for everything else we do. However, this is only possible if we have a personal relationship with God. Just as a child runs to his loving father when something has happened, or if the child is happy about something, God wants us to come to Him with all our cares and worries, and of course with our joy.

He also said there is only one access to God the Father, and that is through His Son, Jesus. He came about two thousand years ago to us. He died for the sins of men, that we might be free and our sins forgiven. God the Father is holy and can't tolerate any sin near Him. Therefore, we should no longer live for ourselves, but to entrust our lives to Jesus; then He will cleanse us by his Holy Spirit, piece by piece and change us for the better. Through Jesus Christ we have access to God the Father. So we go from "minus" to "plus".

Then the seminar leader said: If we take this step and entrust Jesus with our lives, He would remove all the burdens from our shoulders, and free us from all our worries. If Jesus is the Lord in our lives, we would also be awarded with eternal life with God in Heaven - and according to the Bible, there is nothing better! Everyone has eternal life automatically, but it is with Satan from birth because he is the ruler of this world. Only through Jesus are we given access to Heaven where it is eternally awesome and where we lack nothing.

* * *

After the first day of the seminar, we went to our room in total agitation. We could not sleep and were awake a long time. We thought about all the things the speaker had said, and we talked about it. Finally, at 1:00 a.m. in the morning, we came to a conclusion and prayed: "Dear God, if everything we heard today is true and You are real, then give us a clear sign. Wake us up in the morning at 6:00. The man today gave us credible assurance that with You everything is possible, so please wake us up at 6:00 a.m. If we wake up exactly at 6:00 am, then we will know that we are in the right place and that You are real. If we wake up later, then we will pack our bags in the morning and go home! "

When I awoke the next morning, my first look was at my watch. 6:01 a.m.! A minute late, so I told my wife, let's go home! But Sylvia had a hotel clock next to her where it was exactly 6:00 a.m. God had actually awakened us up exactly at 6:00 am! This was for us a clear sign of God, since it was highly unlikely after only a few hours of sleep for us to wake up exactly at 6:00 a.m.

With this clear sign, we started the second day of the seminar. Sometime during the day, the seminar leader asked if anyone wanted to commit their life to Jesus so that He could guide us into the future and give us eternal life with Him. Sylvia and I no longer hesitated even one minute to complete the most important step of our lives! The manager asked us to pray the following prayer, wholeheartedly:

"Jesus, we come before You and confess that we are sinners and have led a sinful life. Please forgive us our trespasses and sins. We have realized that we are not able to cope with our own lives. That's why we give our lives and everything that we are and have, into Your hands and ask that You lead us from now on and show us the right way. We thank You for it. Amen."

After this prayer, from that day forward, the loads of problems, burdens and everything else left me. I felt free and I could laugh for the first time after a long time. The constant anxiety had gone away - and my wife and I were together and hugged and kissed for the first time in a

42

long time! The rest of the seminar was a dream for us. We had so much joy in our hearts that we were "on cloud nine".

* * *

On this "cloud nine" we traveled home and arrived there full of joy and love. We immediately told our children and other family members, explaining what had happened in the last three days. Strangely, they gave us weird looks and could not understand nor believe that a change had taken place in us. Each rolled their eyes when we said we had entrusted our lives to Jesus. However, no one could deny that I, unlike my hitherto mostly grim face, now had a joyful, relaxed appearance.

Of course, I thought that all the stress, the rush, and the many problems with the company were now solved, but this was not the case. However, the morning-prayer time with Sylvia in which we thanked God for everything and gave Him all our cares and concerns, helped me a lot. I felt lighter and ready for the day. Prayer felt completely different than before!

Every morning we read the Bible together, the written Word of God. With the children we prayed also - morning, evening and before meals. The children were surprised, and they followed our lead without any serious discussion because they saw that something had changed to the positive, especially in me. The situation in the company remained unchanged, but our relationship with God grew stronger. God also granted that our marriage was again a real marriage.

My enthusiasm about God and the positive change in Sylvia and me was something I just couldn't hide. At every opportunity, I told everyone how we had found the living faith and what God had changed in our hearts.

* * *

When I had some time to reflect on my life, I realized how often God saved me repeatedly from certain death: There was the first accident when I was four years old, many car accidents, motorcycle accidents - most could have been fatal! That made me even more grateful for God's protection.

Whenever possible, it became the most important task in my life to tell people what's most important: to know where to spend eternity after death - with God, where there are no worries, hardships, pain, disease, war, or hatred. In short: with God, ugliness and evil no longer exist, and we are free from Satan's eternal damnation.

As I write this book, I follow the daily news about Michael Schumacher's health (he is Germany's most successful Formula 1 race car driver) after his devastating ski accident; he is 16 days in a coma as of this writing. According to press reports he is a billionaire, but all the money in the world and the world's best doctors can't heal him. He had the same experience as the title of this book: "From 100 to 0 in 1 second." Nobody knows what will happen tomorrow; we do not even know what happens in a second. Has Michael Schumacher signed up for the free life insurance "Jesus"? Does he know where he would go, if he dies now?

Access to Heaven cannot be bought with all the money in the world, but Jesus has paid for it with his painful death on the cross and now He gives it to us for free. He stretches out his hand to us, we only need to grasp it, that's our job and our choice.

* * *

Because I constantly talk about God and Jesus, and am unable to stop, my youngest brother Markus with his wife from Delitzsch were so surprised about my positive change, they decided to visit the same Seminar "Management with God". Both of them started their personal relationship with Jesus.

I was always in regular phone contact with my oldest brother in the United States. We exchanged our problems, concerns, wishes and dreams in the companies and our personal lives. After I became a believer, I called Werner in my state of euphoria and told him that I had a solution for his problems! I told him that my wife and I had entrusted our lives to Jesus and exactly how we arrived at the experience. It was as if someone had taken a huge, heavy bag off our backs. Werner could not believe what I told him, but expressed great interest. Four weeks later, he told me that he and his wife had also invited Jesus to take over their lives.

In this way, almost the entire extended family gradually gave their lives to Jesus. In my enthusiasm, I even went so far as to invite our closest employees (about 40 people) for dinner in a restaurant followed by a speech about "Management with God" with the same speaker we had in Switzerland. My sister, Regina and her husband came. Her husband did not want to come at all and was totally against it. He even attacked my sister verbally and implied he didn't want to go because I became crazy. For some reason, only God knows why both of them appeared for the special evening.

I saw my brother in-law from afar. I saw his anger and it was obvious he didn't want to attend the event at all. He appeared to feel totally uncomfortable, and I had the feeling that if he would have exploded if the speaker had said one wrong word. But it all went well.

Towards the end of his presentation, the speaker asked who wanted to entrust his life to Jesus. To my great surprise, my brother-in-law said he would do it. Without a sign of disgust or anger, he prayed before all who were present the same prayer we had prayed months ago. His mood, his attitude were transformed completely, and all of his anger had blown over. At the end of the evening, he and my sister departed in total unity, full of love, joy and peace with one another.

* * *

My father was a strong critic of our new faith. He even mentioned we would join a sect! It bothered him the most that I decided almost overnight not to go to the chapel anymore, and to no longer participate in the Rosary. Until then, I had gone to the chapel for prayer almost every Sunday for 25 years. My father had faithfully attended chapel for about 55 years by that time.

He just couldn't understand why I could change after such a long time and not pray the Rosary anymore. I told him over and over again that I now pray to God the Father and to Jesus because I had a personal relationship with Them. Why should I pray to the "Mother of God" to beg God for me? There was actually a statue of the mother Mary above the altar in the chapel where we had prayed. I told him: "That would be the same as if I, your son, would always go to mother when I needed something and ask her if she would ask you instead of going directly to you, my father. Wouldn't you as my father feel bad if I never came to you directly, and what kind of relationship would that be?" He couldn't hear it often enough, I had to explain it to my father again and again, but he wouldn't understand. He saw that a large part of the family had also taken this step to Jesus. This made him more depressed and dismissive. I told him: "You can unload all your worries and problems when you invite Jesus into your life." He will set you free but my father couldn't believe it.

One Sunday, I visited him at home, as so often before. I was about to say goodbye so he could go to pray the Rosary in the chapel, but to my amazement, he and my mother told me that they weren't going to pray the Rosary anymore. They had practiced that tradition for 55 years! It was another miracle. A little later they gave their lives to Jesus.

* * *

At the company, the staff noticed that I had changed. One day, our bookkeeper had to meet with the branch manager in Dresden to discuss new set ups and procedures since she was responsible for the payroll.

I went to Dresden every week in my schedule, so it was only logical that the bookkeeper should come along with me. Unfortunately, all the employees knew that I was a very fast and aggressive driver. If the highway was not busy, I had the reputation of driving 150 miles per hour. That was the standard for my driving and it was not a problem to do that with my BMW.

The employee knew how I usually drove, and she

probably didn't sleep so well the night before we went to Dresden. She didn't know that upon starting my life with Jesus, my driving style had drastically changed. I drove at normal speeds and according to the road conditions.

After returning from Dresden, the bookkeeper told me that my different driving style had convinced her that my new way with Jesus really caused a positive change. A short time later, she ventured with her husband into a new life with Jesus. She was not the only one; in the following months, other staff members made the same decision.

9 From 100 to 0 in 1 Second, Part Two

Despite the radical change of our faith and the associated personal change for the better, the company had not changed very much: the hustle and bustle was common and so were the many problems from morning to night. I prayed more than ever: "Father, only You have a solution to all these problems, therefore, not my will but Your will shall be done!" However, what happened next, we did not understand at all; only much later did we realize that this was really God perfect plan for us.

One day in the mid-1990s at exactly 10:00 a.m., about 50 tax collectors stormed our office building and all the private rooms of our house at the main office in Wimmental. At the same time, tax collectors stormed the offices in our branches in Delitzsch, Dresden and Berlin. This was done to prevent us removing or eliminating any documents. They also wanted to prevent the exchange of information and communication between offices.

The lead investigator told me the authorities suspected us of deliberately evading taxes on our subcontractors. The search of our company and all subsidiaries had the sole purpose of securing evidence.

We as a family and the staff were totally shocked about everything and we were especially shocked about the way we were treated: We felt like criminals, even though we had handled our business properly and cleanly to the best of our knowledge - at least so we thought. After a few days we received a letter from the tax authorities, with the following content:

"Having considered all the documents seized, we came to the conclusion that the company Stark GmbH with its three branches intentionally evaded taxes by using so-called subcontractors hired for bogus contracts. We determined that the subcontractors worked by precise instructions for the company Stark. The subcontractors did not pay any tax, as it is normal for self-employed entrepreneurs. For this reason, we consider all of them employed subcontractors as bogus self-employed and therefore are all employees of the Stark company. We urge you to pay us the evaded taxes amounting to DM 1.8 million (approximately $900,000 U.S.) within two weeks to one of our accounts below. If you fail to pay, we will conduct appropriate enforcement action without further warning. "

That hit us all, of course, like a blow; we knew we would never be able to pay the horrendous amount. We could have said now: "Where are you, God, and if you are there, why did You let this happen?" Interestingly, this message had just the opposite effect on all of the rest of the family who had a personal relationship with God, and they turned even more than ever before Him in prayer, and were pleading to God for help, guidance and direction. Everyone knew: Only God can free us from this situation.

* * *

In consultation with our tax advisors, we successfully negotiated with the tax authorities to defer payment. We could calmly weigh the options and discuss the way forward. At the same time, we prayed incessantly, and asked God to perform a miracle or give us wisdom on

50

how to resolve the situation.

The Word of God says: Our plans are not God's plans and His plans are not ours. Everything that happened was never our plan, but God's plan - and in retrospect, we can say: It was much better for all of us.

We left no stone unturned to save the company. Sadly, all conversations with the tax authorities were unsuccessful. We were allowed to repeatedly defer payment, so we were at least spared enforcement measures. And, we were able to carry on with our normal business – never knowing if we could save the company from bankruptcy.

One morning during my prayer time, I had the impression that we should play the lottery. The lottery win at the time was eight million, so the net from that sum could solve all of our problems at once. I shared the idea with my wife and family. The following weekend, we played Lotto in a total state of euphoria – and we were disappointed when we found out that we didn't win anything!

Later I realized that God had not spoken that morning to me; it had been my wishful thinking and my great despair. If we had better knowledge of the Bible, we would have realized that gambling is not God's idea.

After nearly a year of relentless struggles and prayer, we felt that it was probably God's will to declare bankruptcy. All family members who held leading positions in the company had signed guarantees in recent years, so their personal assets were guarantees for corporate loans.

* * *

Since my wife and I both had no other income, we were not able to pay our monthly payment for the loan on our house that we had built only a few years earlier. Our credit cards were blocked, our private accounts seized, including saving accounts, and my company car was impounded. All this took place a few weeks after we declared bankruptcy for the company. It was the same for all the family members who were involved with the company. Even my father was affected even though he was now only a clerk in the company, but he also had signed personal guarantees for corporate loans.

So came the day when my wife said to me on a Sunday morning: "We have very little cash, I do not know how to feed us and the children tomorrow."

I breathed first a few deep breaths before answering: "The Bible says if we believe in God, as his children, He will make sure that we always have enough food and clothing. I believe what the word of God says, and the Lord will supply for us. "

Then, as with every Sunday, we drove to church with the car loaned to us by my wife's parents. On the way I had the impression that we should give everything we had in cash in the offering basket. I thought, if I tell that my wife, she is going to collapse! Therefore, I didn't want to tell her-- but then I took all my courage and told her softly and gently, what I had in mind. And Sylvia just looked at me and said, "Me, too." So we both emptied our purses completely into the collection plate and went back home without a penny.

As we emptied the mailbox the next day, there was a letter from my brother, Werner. The envelope contained five hundred dollars and a short note that God had instructed him to send this amount to us. We could not believe it! Of course, we were pleased that Werner had sent us the money, but the joy about our Father in Heaven was overwhelming. He really kept what He has promised! God also arranged the perfect timing: The letter had to be sent at the perfect time in order to make sure it arrived at exactly the right day, namely, when we needed it most.

A few days later, we received a call from a Christian businessman, whom we had met only a few weeks ago. He wished to invite Sylvia and me to dinner because he had something to discuss with us. Of course, we gladly accepted the invitation.

The restaurant was very nice and simply pleasant. At dinner he asked us if we would accept something, if we knew that it was from God. I replied: "Of course, if it is from God, we will take it!" He then handed us an envelope and said, God had instructed him to give it to us. We opened the envelope - and found $2000 DM ($1,000 U.S.) in cash!

My wife was crying and I was speechless. Full of joy, we thanked him very much, but he only replied: "Do not thank me, but thank the Lord. I do only what He has told me to do." Then he suggested that since it was Christmas season, we should take some of the money to buy our kids Christmas presents (with whom we had already agreed that they wouldn't get presents that year).

In so many ways, the Lord showed that He has all power in Heaven and on Earth, and that even though He has the whole world under control, He also takes care of our own personal concerns, and in ways that we could never imagine. Within three days, the Lord had given us $2500 DM ($1,250 U.S.)!

We fully realized that His word is true and that in every detail He knows us and He knows our needs: Just in time we had received more than we needed! In our evening prayer, we expressed to Him our enthusiasm with tears of joy. Subsequently, we received in this way several thousand Deutsch Mark.

* * *

Things took their course. The dream house we had built representing our ideas and wishes only a few years earlier was auctioned off. So were the houses belonging to my sister and to our parents who were over seventy years of age. In this difficult time, our parents survived solely due to their strong faith in the Lord. In old age, they had to leave their spacious home and the familiar Wimmental where they had both lived from birth. They had to move into a rental apartment twenty kilometers away. Everything was different; at more than seventy years old, our parents started from scratch. When I think about how they handled all that happened to them: Hats off!

We also had to move; at least we could stay in Wimmental. The main question in our prayer requests was: Lord, what do You want us to do? What is Your plan for us? How and where should we make money now?

For Sylvia, God soon opened a door: She went to work for our former accountant doing the accounting for some of his clients. I had a strong urge to help small, struggling companies in need. As CEO of Stark GmbH, I had acquired enormous knowledge; the last year before the bankruptcy was especially very influential and educational for me. That's why I wanted to serve small businesses and entrepreneurs with my experience and knowledge.

Word spread quickly about me, and soon I had my first client. Most of my clients had small businesses, most of them were excellent craftsmen, but they had their problems with office work and business processes. Their God-given talents lay more in the craft and not so much in the business sector.

For example: one craftsman was always overdrawn, and he received very nasty calls from his bank. I scheduled an appointment with the bank to introduce myself and to explain to the bank that I would come up with a business plan for our mutual client if the bank would give us a little bit more time. This gave us some time to create an actual analysis. I informed the bank once a week about the current state of affairs and the measures already taken. The bankers calmed down and our efforts improved the business relationship between the bankers, my clients and me.

The next step was the completion of the initial analysis. I did this with the help of my wife, who brought the bookkeeping up to date on an hourly basis for the small business. It turned out that my client forgot to send out invoices for finished work. No wonder he was in the red! I made sure that the customers were billed as soon as possible. My client was respected by all of their customers and was popular with them. I made him call them, especially to ask them for immediate payment. This was not easy, but I helped him to make the calls. My wife booked each payment received immediately, so everyone had the best possible overview of the business.

This measure alone significantly improved the cash flow situation for my client, which immediately showed positive cash flow on the bank account. The bankers' point of view changed and they became very friendly again with my client.

After posting all invoices, it became clear that many customers had not paid my clients. We sent immediate reminders for overdue bills. I also asked my clients to call these customers and ask them to kindly pay the overdue bill. Furthermore, I kept the bank up-to-date. Through these confidence-building measures, the relationship with the bank improved.

I was able to help many small business owners through my own experience and thanks to the help of my wife. I tried to keep my consultation fee for my clients as low as possible according to the company's situation.

However, my support of a struggling company/client was not limited to practical measures. Before each consultation, I clearly told them about my faith in God. I told my clients that I could not solve all their problems, but that God could. I explained that I was only God's instrument. If we asked Him together in prayer for His wisdom, guidance and direction, He would lead us so that we could take the right measures and bring the sinking ship back on its feet. This point was particularly important to me; and I wanted to have 100% agreement with my clients on this topic.

10 Man Proposes and God Disposes

Finding that God is wonderful and powerful, many people in our immediate environment found a living relationship with God. In our life of faith, the Lord led us further and opened new doors: Through a friend we learned of an association called "Christian businessmen". Usually once a month, they hosted an event, not in a Christian community center, but in a nice restaurant with a meeting room.

The evening was called "Chapter" and usually began with a meal. Afterward, the guest speaker would report the facts about his life without God, by what circumstances he had found God, and how God had changed his life - always very radically for the better. Often the guest speakers were themselves entrepreneurs, which was especially interesting for me! They discussed topics such as "Why does God allow that?" Or "God wants you to live".

At the end of the first evening, Sylvia and I absolutely loved the event, the guest speaker, the people we met, and the organizers. We did not need to think about it – for it was clear that we would register for the next meeting, to be held a month later at the same time in the same place. Soon we were "regulars". It was not long before I was an active member of the Heilbronn Chapter.

At the end of the 1990's, there were such events in almost every major city in Germany, with a total of about 150 local groups. One day, I was asked if I would like to become a speaker, because of my story about my many accidents and my experience with the decline of my company, and also my radical change after the total capitulation before God. It would certainly interest many people a lot. I had to discuss it with Sylvia, and I talked to God about it. When I felt that I had peace in my heart, and with my health, and had Sylvia's approval, I said yes.

It was not long before I had to handle the first session of questions and answers. My speaking events started in southern Germany. During the Chapter events, I asked my wife to report from her point of view. This particularly appealed to the women and it made our story much more interesting. We received more and more invitations for chapter speaker, and very soon we were traveling all over Germany 2-3 times a month.

My speeches always had the same structure: I started by reporting our lives to the point where we had found God. Then, I explained what God had done, how He changed our lives, and what miracles He had done for us. Finally, I encouraged the audience to engage in a personal relationship with God.

* * *

Since I was an entrepreneur, I was especially interested in company owners in my audience. I found that many of them were not Christians. I also knew they needed God because they had so much responsibility for their employees, customers, suppliers, banks, and their own families. They needed a living faith in God to lead their companies responsibly and biblically, and to guide the workers well. I am convinced that if the boss of a company is leading according to Biblical standards, they are not deceiving anyone, they are being true, and loving their neighbor as themselves. This will inevitably have a positive effect on their employees, customers and suppliers.

The Word of God says, if we act according to the commandments of God, our affairs will be blessed and thus be successful. I believe my desire to start a new chapter came from God. I decided to concentrate on a chapter exclusively for business owners. The goal was to show such people how to give their businesses and, in particular, their private lives to Jesus, so that He could carry the whole burden and take over the leadership in all areas of their lives.

My vision interested seven entrepreneurs and they had the same desire. We met each week to exchange ideas and to pray together, asking God what and how He wanted us to get started. More ideas were added to each meeting, and our vision became a little clearer each time. We started with regular meetings every second month, and we invited only business people. The events were very well attended.

Through speeches or in personal conversations, many business people found answers. They discovered how problems could be solved by faith in God, in the Word of God, and in the Bible.

* * *

It was not enough, however. In addition to my duties as head of the local group in Ludwigsburg for "Christian Businessmen" and as the area manager for Baden-Württemberg and Rhineland-Pfalz, God opened up another field for me. I had been active in the Choir since my youth. A member of the first choir board wanted to resign for reasons of age. He said the choir needed young blood. He expressed that I would certainly be the right person for this post.

I thanked him for his confidence - after all, the association had 35 active singers and more than 300 passive members. Once again, I wanted to talk with my wife first and pray to God with her.

It was very important for me to have God's approval! It was clear to me that this task would also take more of my time. I already had a few other obligations; I also worked as a company consultant. I could only do all the additional tasks in peace if God agreed. Sylvia and I felt at peace with God, which was primary in our lives. So, I accepted and was proposed as the new head of the choir.

The choir Committee was divided. There had been a discussion in the village about how much I had changed since I had come to my faith in God. Some were afraid that I would use my position and convert the whole club to my sect, or at least that was the rumor. A meeting was arranged to clarify the issue. After I promised not to evangelize the members, I was elected as the new head of the choir Urbanus Wimmental.

As the head of the choir, I experienced God's guidance and blessing. I prayed a lot for the association, and God made overwhelming changes. The conductor, who had done an excellent job for many years, wanted to resign for reasons of age. In search of a successor, we found a young and motivated conductor. He knew how to inspire and motivate both the younger and the older singers with new, fresh, and modern songs.

Our first public performances under his direction earned us much praise and approval, and not only in the press. Our repertoire was something special in the area and attracted a lot of young people. Soon we had sixty active singers!

In the surrounding villages there were no kids' choirs, so "Urbanus Kids" was founded on my suggestion. The parents and their children were enthusiastic. At times, under the guidance of Sylvia, forty happy children sang their hearts out. Sylvia and our new choir director were especially pleased to see how well the children developed, how they felt, how they lost their shyness, how they loved to sing, and enjoyed the rehearsals.

Shortly afterwards, the youth choir for teenagers "Young Generation" was added, and our concerts always had a nice triangle. The "Urbanus Kids" started the concerts, then the "Young Generation" took over, and finally the adult choir finished the rest of the evening. We always had a full house, and sometimes it was even overcrowded. The concerts were huge fun with all the parties!

Kevin, our youngest child, also sang in the Children's Choir and did so well that he was usually allowed to perform solo as a prelude. The tremendous change in the club, which one could call an explosion, was particularly welcome. I saw what God could do and it was clear to me that our success was not due to my performance, nor the performance of the committee or the conductor. It was primarily God's blessing. He brought the right people together at the right time and that made our success possible.

Of course, God uses humans to do His work. God is the

initiator and when we trust Him, He creates change, and always for the good. That is why I give God thanks and praise for all that He does.

11 In the Land of Limited Opportunities

As an accountant in the tax office and in our consulting company, and as a housewife, wife, mother, and as a volunteer in the children's choir, Sylvia was well employed. I, too, was not neglected: My business consulting, the honorary posts as Chapter & Area Manager in "Christian Businessmen", as well as head of Urbanus choir, kept me on my toes. Sylvia and I generally started our day early in the morning with prayer time, and I still had my own personal time with God.

Early one morning in April 2001 during my personal time with the Lord, the thought came to me that we should emigrate to the U.S.A. It certainly was not my idea! After the total decline we had suffered, our lives and our routines had somewhat returned to normal: Sylvia and I each had a job that was fun, we felt comfortable in our rented home, and also our extra activities each week were developing well.

There was only one reason why I did not immediately reject this idea: It had come to me in an "audience with God". Therefore, it was possible that God had put this idea to me. It would certainly not have been the first time that God had given me an idea or an answer. So, I thought carefully about it and decided the plan should be given a chance. I asked God for confirmation: "God, if this is not from You – as the lottery idea was not from You, then let me forget it. But if it is from You, then let it get stronger in my heart.

* * *

Emigration thoughts became stronger. I talked to no one about it, and one morning I prayed, "Lord, if it really is Your plan for us to emigrate to America, then please prepare my family for it. My wife, our three sons, Sylvia's parents and my own Parents should all agree. Should one of them be against it, I will take that as a sign that emigration is not Your way for us. "

Now I thought excitedly: 'When would all of the family be ready for it?' I did not want to open discussions and try to persuade Sylvia's parents, knowing that Sylvia had a really close relationship with them. On the other hand, I was more and more pleased about the idea of emigrating. I didn't want to "sell" Sylvia on the idea to move to the U.S., for I wanted it to be her choice also. I especially wanted to be able to talk and consult with Sylvia about it. It was an inner struggle for me.

At the end of April, we were traveling down the road with all five of us in the car (Sylvia, our sons and I). We were all together and no one had somewhere else to go. I asked: "Lord, is now the time?"

I gathered my courage and asked everybody, "What would you all think if we were to emigrate to the U.S.?" The three boys were immediately thrilled, and my wife joined the teenagers right away without any hesitation.

Our parents agreed; they even encouraged us. The first hurdle had been cleared, but there was more to be done. I was glad we were united in the decision and could share the upcoming tasks together! As a family we prayed: "Dear God, this is a serious decision. Please encourage my brother, Werner to agree to employ us in his company in the U.S. And please allow everything to go well with the American consulate in order to get a work visa, at least for a year. "

* * *

I called Werner and presented him with my thoughts. Of course, he had to discuss it with his wife. After a few days, he gave the green light, and at the beginning of May 2001, we sent the Visa applications to the Consulate. Processing usually took six to eight weeks, so we expected the Visas to arrive at the end of June or beginning of July. But to our surprise, we received the Visas in early June! Not only that: the Visas were for five years – not just one year! Without a personal interview, just like that, and for five years! How did it come to this? We didn't have to puzzle over it for long. We knew: God had a hand in it!

The Bible says that God knows the end before the beginning. So He knew that we would stay in the U.S. longer, and not for just one year. For us, this was an additional confirmation from God.

Many friends encouraged us. One couple, for example, called us; they had prayed for us and God showed them a Bible verse, stating: " The Lord said to Abram: Leave your country, your family, and your relatives and go to the land that I will show you." (Genesis 12:1). So we received a lot of clear confirmations from friends and family, which made for joy in our hearts during all the preparations.

It was good that the visas had come so quickly, for it gave us enough time. There were so many tasks to regulate - to complete consultations and cancel contracts, handle and transfer honorary positions and instruct followers. We had to empty the apartment, pack our bags and prepare for the container in which we would ship part of our furniture and other important goods. We also had think about the future education of the children. And finally, we had to organize a big farewell party for family and friends. The time passed quickly and soon we were at the end of August.

* * *

And then we were sitting in the plane, with mixed feelings and heavy hearts, but also with anticipation for the new. The last few months had demanded a lot out of us. We only wanted to relax and recover for three weeks in Florida while our container was in route. Then, we wanted to settle in Huntsville, Alabama.

One of the strongest first impressions we received while on vacation was with the TV. There were over one hundred television stations with a huge selection! One morning, we were truly amazed about the kinds of action movies they showed on TV. There was an airplane flying and then crashing into a skyscraper in broad daylight! It is still unbelievable today: This event was not a feature film, however, as we soon learned. It was a real event happening in New York, in our new homeland, and it was probably a terrorist attack. It was the date that became known in history as 9/11. In shock, we forgot all about the sunshine and swimwear!

For the next few hours, we sat and watched television. Our heads were shaking and we couldn't believe our eyes: Who could plan and execute such a terrible thing? We were baffled. What could we do except pray?

According to news reports, several thousand people were killed and many were injured; the broadcasters repeatedly called for blood donations. We wanted to help, so we went into the town center to donate blood. And again, we couldn't believe our eyes: there were hundreds of prospective donors waiting! After a long wait, it was finally our turn. Unfortunately, we were sent away with the explanation that the blood banks were only allowed to take the blood of American citizens who had not lived outside the country. However, the blood bank lady thanked us many times and we could feel how much she appreciated our wish to donate blood and to help.

During the days that followed, we saw how the American people stood together as one, regardless of color or religion. We listened to the address by President George W. Bush on TV. At the end of his speech, he called on the American people for constant prayer, and he stated that now only God could help. Once again we saw that Americans responded immediately and it was overwhelming: there were special worship and prayer times scheduled and the churches were crowded. The unity and awareness to be totally dependent on God was an awesome experience; unfortunately, it lasted only a few weeks before people resumed their routines.

During that time, we also realized that God always has perfect timing: If we had entered the U.S. just two weeks later, we would have been denied entry. After 9-11-2001, allowing foreigners into the United States totally stopped. If I remember correctly, the entirety of all air traffic across the country was also shut down for two days, another historical "first" for the aviation and travel industry.

God knows everything. He made sure that our visa applications were processed unusually fast just so we could enter before September 11. The date "9/11" will always remain in my memory - and thus also the time we arrived in the "New World".

* * *

Not long after the attacks of 9/11, we drove to Huntsville, Alabama to settle in and take root. With Werner's help, we were able to rent a house relatively quickly, enroll the children in school and get used to the "American Way of Life". The new beginning was very difficult; everything was so unfamiliar. Due to the language barrier, things were particularly difficult. My English, which I had studied in the German school 25 years ago, simply no longer existed. Sylvia was a lot better in English, and she had to constantly interpret.

One day, Sylvia became totally overwhelmed and with tears in her eyes said: "I want to go home!" I will never forget that day. There was nothing for us anymore in Germany -- no home and hence no turning back. Our home was here now! I was thankful that God had given us so many signs. We knew for certain that here was our new place to be. It was our new home. This knowledge didn't make our path any easier, however.

Against all odds, we acclimated gradually. A large church in Huntsville offered a free English course, which helped me a lot. I learned to actually communicate at a reasonable level, so I took the job as "General Manager" in my brother's company. The company had a tile/stone showroom, a fabrication shop where we made granite and marble countertops for kitchens and bathrooms, an installation department for the installation of our

68

countertops, and tile setters installed the materials we sold in the showroom.

My wife had years of experience in accounting in Germany. So, she took over the bookkeeping and gradually became familiar with the new type of accounting. In particular, payroll was totally new territory for Sylvia because the rules were quite different than in Germany.

So much was new for me also, even though my life's business was in tiles. In America, the tiles were the quality as those in Germany, and they do cost money, but those were the only things in common between the two countries when it came to the tile business.

So, Sylvia and I both had a real hard time at the beginning. It was good that God was on our side and He never left us alone. That helped us the most. We found our way back to our usual early morning-prayer routine, and prayed again in the evening before bedtime. We could feel how the Lord helped us during that time. So all the unusual things in our lives soon became the routine.

* * *

And we learned the customs of this country — many of them were pleasant, but other customs and rules shocked me. For example, the U.S. only permits a speed limit of 70 miles per hour on a three-lane highway even with no traffic. It was a surprise to me. Seventy miles per hour is 115 km per hour in Germany, and I was used to driving at least 180 km per hour, which is 115 miles per hour. In America, everything is a long distance in comparison to Germany. I considered it a positive that one could pass cars on the left as well as on the right and not have to be held back in the right lane by a slow-moving car on the left.

We enjoyed the fact that we could go shopping in supermarkets 24/7, around the clock, including Sundays. And, we were delighted to see a supermarket chain advertise that if one could get their products cheaper elsewhere, they would reduce their prices accordingly to match the lower price.

Another big surprise: Even in the computer age, one could pay all regular bills by check if one so chooses, whether for business or personal bills. We found it interesting, new and convenient to experience the "drive-through". One could order from the car, whether for fast-food restaurants, at banks or at pharmacies. It was amazing to us that anything could be delivered to our car --food, bank deposits/withdrawals, and even prescription medicines!

Huntsville is full of churches. There are over a hundred churches, and many have two or three Sunday services, plus one on Wednesday night. Just for comparison: Our town of Heilbronn has only 40 churches instead of over a hundred, even though Heilbronn is almost the same size as Huntsville!

Also striking was the friendliness of the people. At work, I often experienced a customer calling to tell us how satisfied he was with the quality of work, especially with the installers. In other businesses, when we gave the impression that we were looking for something, people approached us immediately wanting to know if they could help us. It was a level of customer service we had not seen before, and the clients whom we served in our own business were equally appreciative.

In restaurants, the servers were very attentive. In the restaurant and service industries, the basic salary of employees is generally really low, so they needed to earn tips. Therefore, they were always very friendly and accommodating to get the highest possible tip.

* * *

In the craft, it is slightly different; the quality of the work varies extremely and is very often below German quality work. This is probably one reason why my brother's company is successful. Werner is so picky and trains all installers in the German way. The installers know if they don't do a 100% perfect job, they would have to redo it. So, in order to avoid the redo, they do it correctly from the beginning. Hence, the probable reason why German car manufacturers are also so high in demand in the U.S. Americans who drive a German car choose one because they know the quality and the performance of German engineering. Car owners would rather pay the higher price for quality, and get more money in return upon resale of the car.

We found many positive differences between our new homeland and our old homeland, and we also found things that were not so good.

12 Food, Drinks, Poison

When we left Germany, there were only two fast-food restaurants in Heilbronn. In Huntsville, there were over a hundred of them! Both cities have about the same size population. With so many restaurants and the lower prices than in Europe, it was easy for us to adapt to the customary dietary style. We learned that many Americans don't cook very often because the food is so inexpensive in restaurants. We also discovered the benefits of eating out inexpensively because it saved us a lot of time for more important things.

Thanks to our new eating habits, I gained 24 pounds in a few months. I decided I needed to change my fluid consumption. Instead of "normal" Cola or Sprite (400 kilocalories) I began drinking the diet version (zero calories). Also, I decided to eat less, skip breakfast and go jogging in the morning for half an hour.

Nevertheless, I didn't lose weight. On the contrary, I had to fight to avoid gaining more weight. I also had an upset stomach, headache, malaise and diarrhea. I wondered: what is wrong with me?

A pattern of years of being overweight and having health problems began to create serious mental problems. In the meantime, I became a good customer of the pharmacy. Then God had mercy and little by little showed me, and the whole family, the real cause of our poor health. As my English improved, I began to read everything I could on the subject.

Only one goal

I believe that many large companies in the food industry have only one goal: achieve the highest profits in the shortest time possible without regard to human beings, their health and even their lives. I suspect that part of their huge profit is used to directly influence the government to make sure laws are passed for the convenience of the food companies. . In an article written by attorney Jonathan W. Emord entitled "FDA Violation of the Rule of Law", a description of the 1962 Kefauver-Harris Drug Amendments reveals how the FDA protects the drug industry. (Emord, 2006)

In Germany, I knew of food protection laws. The German government assures us that the foods offered are not harmful and can be consumed without hesitation. If a German food manufacturer produced something harmful for the people, he would get severely punished and would have to pay huge fines. As a citizen, I expect the government to protect the quality of our food.

It is different in the U.S. There is the Food & Drug Administration called the F.D.A., but apparently they don't oppose some harmful ingredients that are very bad for people. I now understand why many U.S. foods are banned in Europe and aren't allowed to be sold. Such bans upset the food industry, as I read in Susanna Kim's article "11 Food Ingredients Banned Outside the U.S. That We Eat" (Kim, 2013). Another interesting book is "Inside the FDA: The Business and Politics behind the Drugs We Take and the Food We Eat" (Hawthorne, 2005). A reviewer of the book, Gregory Conko of Competitive Enterprise Institute, points out that private societies, insurance plans, the American Medical Society, and others are able to certify new drugs (Conko, 2007).

Some politicians are well aware that the F.D.A. has restrictions on its obligations; the food manufacturers know it also and manage to do what they want. Sometimes it appears that food corporations, the politicians, the F.D.A. and the pharmaceutical companies are working all together. It seems quite logical: Sometimes really bad, contaminated, or toxic foods make people sick; so they need more prescriptions and over-the-counter drugs to get well again. In the end, everybody except the consumer benefits. Some politicians might be receiving incentives and contributions from lobbyists for the food and drug companies. Not enough laws are being passed to protect the public. The pharmacies sell more medications, so they make more money. And it seems that the food companies produce a lot cheaper with less healthy ingredients, and make more money in the process. But, I'm just guessing.

The fact is: In recent years, the cancer rate in the U.S. has risen. In a global comparison with all the other countries in the world, the U.S. reached the 9th highest rate of cancer. (Global Cancer Facts & Figures, 2012). It is even said that within ten years, almost half of Americans will develop some form of cancer. Similar numbers are available for diabetes. In the U.S., there are 23.6 million diabetics, which is the 3rd highest rate in the world. In 1994, the obesity rate was at 18%; it reached 26% in 2010. It is even higher now.

The following are more facts that Sylvia and I have gathered from various sources.

Corn Syrup

A study by the University of California from 2009 shows that the consumption of corn syrup, high fructose content ("high fructose corn syrup," HFCS) is pretty much the fastest way to ruin one's health. Fructose (fruit sugar) is a popular sweetener for the food industry because it has a higher sweetening power than glucose (dextrose), so manufacturers need less of it and it costs less. However, the fructose contained in the corn syrup makes one's body think that one is still hungry so more food is consumed when one is always hungry. Dr. Mark Hyman of the Cleveland Clinic wrote that Americans consume over 60 pounds per year of HFCS (Hyman, 2011).

The human body was created to break down starch into glucose. A ten-week study with 16 volunteers, who deliberately ate high amounts of fructose or HFCS, showed that the body harbored extra fat cells - to the heart, liver and the digestive organs. A comparison group ate normal sugar (made up in equal parts of glucose and fructose), and they had none of these symptoms.

Food manufacturers often use Fructose because it can be obtained by using enzymes from corn, and corn is bountiful in the U.S. It sweetens more; therefore it is less expensive than normal sugar. In the U.S., HFCS is used in all soft drinks as the only caloric sweetener. Even so-called fruit juices are sweetened with it.

Common sense says: I want to drink something healthy, so I buy a fruit juice. But few know that this "juice" is diluted with water, then unhealthy colors, flavors and, indeed, high fructose corn syrup are added to achieve a nice color and taste, resulting in harm to the body, instead of good.

More than two thirds of all the foods in this country contain HFCS; besides beverages, almost all baked goods, cereal, yogurt, chocolate, chocolate bars - and even beer contains HFCS, which I can't understand at all. Is that the cause of the "beer belly"? There is actually no American beer without HFCS! I would like to point out that many beers from other countries contain no HFCS.

Most American bread or rolls contain HFCS, which is not necessary. We baked our own bread, without a single gram of sugar, and yet it tastes great! Incidentally, the average American wheat bread consists of 40 (forty) different ingredients; our homemade wheat bread on the other hand comes out with just four ingredients. Sugar or HFCS are not one of the ingredients.

Sugar — HFCS consumption has risen dramatically in recent decades; the average American ingests well over 2 pounds of sugar/HFCS every week!

Not to mention cakes and biscuits, fruit "juice" and lemonade: Even a small soda bottle (0.33 liters) contains a huge amount of HFCS! I would say in such a magnitude, it is pure poison.

As already mentioned, a high HFCS-use causes the formation of fat cells to the liver and other organs. Our liver struggles to reduce HFCS and converts it into fat, which is stored in the body. If you take in 120 calories of food less than 1 calorie will be stored in the body as fat. If you take in 120 calories in HFCS, 40 calories in fat will be stored.

In addition, the processing of HFCS in the body results in

76

a long list of waste products and toxins, which can lead to hypertension and gout. It also tricks the brain into believing we need more to eat.

The main problem is that HFCS leads to fatty liver, even in people who do not drink a drop of alcohol. With 90 million affected, the non-alcoholic fatty liver disease in the United States has become a widespread disease. The consequences are diseases such as insulin resistance (pre-diabetes, type II diabetes) or diabetes. In addition, HFCS is a major cause of heart attack, stroke and cancer, as well as dementia.

My oldest son Patrick has two sons; once a week they are allowed to go to "Oma and Opa", as they call us in good German. We gave them some sweets like chocolates, candies or the like, but after twenty minutes, both turned into little monsters with an unbelievable amount of energy. We couldn't control them.

At the time, we did not know that all the sweets we gave them contained HFCS instead of sugar, and it is bad enough for an adult body, so a child can hardly manage HFCS. It is said that in comparison to normal sugar, it takes the body three times longer to process HFCS. When we realized it, we stopped giving them candy.

Then something interesting happened. Last year my wife brought a German chocolate bar with her from her trip to Germany. In an unguarded moment, the children saw the chocolate and ate almost all of it. We expected a huge energy attack again, but to our amazement nothing happened. We wondered why? We discovered that the German chocolate contained no corn syrup, but ordinary sugar.

Meat filled with hormones

The American supermarket has even more to offer. For example, hormones: Cows give milk and meat, and the manufacturers say: The more, the better which results in more money. They inject the cows with a synthetic growth hormone, so they grow faster and give ten to twenty percent more milk. This growth hormone is approved by the FDA and is currently the best-selling drug for animals in the U.S. If you are interested, read: "What's in your meat?" (Seattle Organic Restaurants, 2017).

Growth hormone is distributed throughout the body of the animal and it is also in the milk. Therefore, growth hormone is found in all dairy products like butter, yogurt, milkshakes, and cheese.

The result is an increased risk of breast and prostate cancer. Over 30 countries had banned the growth hormone used in American meat and dairy.

In a study of ground beef for hamburgers, eight samples of harmful bacteria, ammonia and growth hormones appeared in the samples. Two samples had parasites.

Chickens are more than twice as large as usual and grow twice as fast when administering them growth hormones. (This applies to other animals as well.)

Earlier in history, arsenic was simply a poison, but a pinch of arsenic in chicken feed gives the meat a healthy color. Supposedly, that is what the consumers want. Millions of people eat chicken daily and now many fast-food restaurants offer chicken burgers and chicken. In the

U.S., chicken has become the most popular type of meat. So the question is: what to do? Perhaps we should become Vegetarians? Most baked goods are made with eggs, but the eggs come from chickens injected with poison, so all products made out of eggs are really unhealthy.

Most American intake poison – a glass of milk or yogurt with breakfast, and through meat, egg noodles or biscuits.

Added to this is the way the animals are raised. Ever heard of the Animal Factory? Yes, the cattle and chickens are treated as if they were on an assembly line and not in a green pasture. Instead they get mostly corn, and sometimes are even fed mechanically with chemically treated carcasses. In 2014, a study showed that over half of the samples of meat showed fecal contamination. (Cummins, 2016).

The cattle vegetate in a confined space where they can't move and is therefore prone to obesity, which consumers wouldn't like at all. Even if consumers wanted to see how their meat is raised, many "animal factories" do not allow visitors, for they know the public would be shocked. Even animal obesity can be regulated: Ractopamine, acted as Paylean or Optaflexx, is well tolerated in cattle, pigs and turkeys in general.

This wonder drug reduces the fat content in meat and strengthens the muscles. Sounds like a fairy tale, but it is true: This type of productive "dietary supplements" will cause cardiovascular diseases and ADS (Attention Deficit Disorder) in consumers like you and me. No wonder the stuff is banned in 160 countries. Many countries, including China and Russia have stopped the import of meat from the USA as of February 2013.

Is fish an alternative? Consider the salmon. The salmon sold in most stores is no longer living in the wild, but is "cultured" in so-called fish farms. Fish farms are a very small space where hundreds of salmon are raised with hazardous chemicals, antibiotics and other drugs, and they get food that is totally unnatural for them but makes them grow really fast. Do you think this is really a healthy food alternative for humans?

Gene Manipulation

The largest food producer in the U.S.A. has come up with something special: In order to make the cultivation of corn and soybeans, as well as wheat, barley and rye effective, these seeds were genetically engineered in the laboratory - the young plants should be resistant to weed killers. Sounds good but, is it?

Once after sowing, the first plants are visible in the fields as are the first weeds. Many miles wide of fields are then sprayed from an airplane with the weed killer "Round Up". The weed dies immediately, and the crop grows since it is genetically modified and resistant against the weed killer. Who wants to know what happens in the long term with the soil contaminated by the weed killer? And what happens when the Round Up gets into the groundwater? Birds and bees are also dying from the use of Neonics and other toxins in our food. (Paul & Cummins, 2014).

Genetically modified corn doesn't have the nutrition God intended. The many unpleasant consequences are still largely unexplored. Tests on rats fed with GMO plants showed injuries to internal organs, gastrointestinal problems, immune system disorders and premature aging. An expert on GMO, Jeff Smith, believes those producing GMO plants need to be held accountable (Smith, 2016).

In humans, chronic diseases have risen from 7% to 13% since the introduction of the GMO; allergies and digestive problems have dramatically increased. What is the FDA doing? The scientists of the FDA are convinced that the consumption of genetically modified organisms is generally harmful to health, and their compatibility must be closely examined. The scientists also expressed concerns that the GMO contains poison and is a leading cause of allergies. One scientist at Harvard, Charles Xu, has written a blog about the effect of GMO on people who suffer from allergies (Xu, 2015).

This information has been shared with politicians, and so far, it has fallen on deaf ears. Politicians and the food industry stated that the GMO changes are necessary to food production and the side effects would be tolerated, so the FDA approved the use of genetically modified seeds.

There is no government-funded, long-term study of the compatibility of genetically modified foods in the United States.

According to reports of several farmers, after feeding GMO to their livestock, the fertility of pigs and cows went down by fifty percent and the miscarriage rate went up substantially. Rats in laboratories that were fed with genetically modified tomatoes, got stomach bleeding and died within two weeks. In Germany, twelve cows died when they were administered GMO feed.

In the 1990s, soy flour and soy products have been touted as a panacea, and soy was considered to prevent breast and prostate cancer. Then the consumption increased explosively, and now soybeans grow in the U.S. on more than 25 million square miles.

Soy contains a lot of protein and oil - in many foods a welcome ingredient. For example, soy is in muesli bars, slimming drinks, fruit "juices", soups, sauces, baked goods, cereals, pizza and much more. The addition of soybean powder increases the protein content of food tremendously, so it is really attractive for bodybuilders.

The advertising is silent on the fact that 95% of the soybean plants are genetically engineered, and GMO soy has unfortunately lost its healing power. Instead, GMO soy increases diseases and makes the human life difficult, creates infertility in men and women, miscarriage, insomnia, digestive problems and food allergies.

I have already mentioned the scary effects of HFCS. Here is an addition: 95% of the U.S. corn harvest is achieved by using GMO. So, 95% of the market HFCS is genetically modified; the already disastrous effects of the synthetic sugar are characterized yet extremely amplified with GMO. I suspect that more than 150 million Americans daily consume GMO high fructose corn syrup - with unforeseeable consequences for their future health.

Although the adverse effects of GMOs are known throughout the world, there are baby food manufacturers that use genetically modified ingredients and claim that this is harmless for babies.

By the way: there will soon be GMO apples. The apple will always have the same taste, the same color, the same size, and the best part: It won't rot. Man can talk of The Apple for eternity.

The Chemical Plant

More than three thousand substances from chemical plants can be found in the United States in our plates: color additives, flavorings, preservatives - even in baby and children's food, which is forbidden in the European Union. Among these additives, there are some that may result in cancer and miscarriage or trigger allergies in children. For example, the food dyes such as "Red 40" (E 129) and "Yellow 6" (E 110).

Some ingredients that are used by the fast food chains in the U.S. are banned in many other countries.

Many diet drinks containing aspartame. This ingredient makes the drink taste sweeter than sugar and is "pure poison", for aspartame causes dementia, depression, joint pain, weight gain, headaches, migraines, dizziness, sight and hearing and smelling - and flavor loss.

Sylvia and I can confirm firsthand many of these effects. As already mentioned, we switched to diet drinks because we wanted to lose weight. Weight loss was not possible on diet drinks; on the contrary, we experienced further weight gain and other impairments, especially migraines, headaches, dizziness and pain in the joints caused by osteoarthritis.

Meanwhile, a new zero-calorie sweetener is on the market. It contains no aspartame and is advertised as natural and does not contain synthesis, and should therefore be very healthy. But even with the new zero-calorie sweetener, the occurrence of, headaches, dizziness, stomach pain, diarrhea, flatulence, kidney problems and other adverse effects were observed in the test.

Ever heard of brominated vegetable oil? You will find it in most sodas or "sports drinks" with lemon flavor, it is called BVO ("brominated vegetable oil"). Unfortunately BVO may cause skin rash, acne, fatigue and cardiac arrhythmias in humans. By the way: BVO is banned in the European Union and in Japan for use in food. Pepsi announced in 2013 that they were removing BVO from Gatorade (Chang, 2014), probably due to side effects.

Pure Water

In the U.S., it is quite normal to drink tap water. In the kitchen at the tap, one can install a filter to assure that the water is healthy to drink. In addition, the city utility administration assures us that they test the water regularly.

But the city does not mention to their citizens that they add a certain proportion of fluoride and chloride to the water supply. Fluoride is contained in toothpaste to serve dental health, which is actually a well-intentioned idea. (Meanwhile, many Americans have health insurance, but few policies cover dental treatment.)

According to the city utilities company, fluoride is not harmful in any way. What is not disclosed is that fluoride can cause brain damage, low IQ, Arthritis, Osteoarthritis, bone cancer and fluoride increases the overall risk of tumors (Connett, 2010). In 90% of all cities in the U.S., drinking water is fluoridated, and I suspect that the majority of households in the U.S. consume fluoridated tap water.

Regular household water filters can't remove fluoride, so we decided to buy our drinking water at the grocery store. That did not work either because it also contains fluoride. We recently learned from our doctor that we have arthritis. Could this have to do with our drinking water??

Anyway, I went in search for fluoride-free water and ended up buying spring water in glass bottles.

For the past few years, we have gathered more and more food information. We have been attentive when shopping. Our sons and daughters have also been watchful. We exchange advice on shopping and nutrition. It almost takes a study to always buy the right goods. Meanwhile, we buy almost exclusively organic products and hope we are buying healthy food.

We are grateful to God that He has opened our eyes to all these things. The Bible says: After God created the world, He looked at everything, "and it was very good." (Genesis 1:31). That means plants, creatures, water, fruit - everything was good.

The soybean plant was good and when supplied to the body in the correct form, can have a healthy effect. So it was with everything created through God in this world. But now Man is trying to act as if he were God, and wants to change what God originally created perfectly. The result is in the evidence, above.

In the U.S. as in Germany, millions of people believe that the foods offered have been tested and are good. Almost everyone believes that no one would knowingly, intentionally offer sickening or poisonous products. Therefore, it is no wonder that so many people look sick; every other person is overweight. I can only pray: "Jesus, help us!!"

How can that be?

The result of my research makes me wonder: How can people be capable of such actions and deliberately conceal all this information, reassure their neighbors to believe that there is no cause for concern, and then watch as our food kills a lot of people, slowly but surely?

Actually, I do not need the answer to this question; I can give the answer myself because twenty years ago I myself was one of them. As head of 400 employees and without a personal relationship with God, I wanted only one thing: to make as much revenue and profit as I can in any way possible. I thought a lot of money, nice cars and homes could fill the void inside of me, but it didn't. I can imagine that this is the same way the bosses of the big food companies act, for it is all about money and profit, no matter what. Jesus said, "Forgive them, Father! They don't know what they are doing." (Luke 23:34)

Thank God, that He opened up my eyes and showed me, in His grace, what really matters in life, what the real value in life is, which is to have a personal relationship with Him and thereby gain eternal life with God in Heaven, not in Hell.

13 Politics and Society

When we had the "Food Science" reasonably digested, the Lord drew our attention to the social and political tendencies of the United States. When it was founded over two hundred years ago, the President of the Continental Congress and other well-known men signed a "Declaration of Independence" which became the foundation for the further development of the country.

The Declaration stated therein:

- Our rights are given to us by God, and they are inalienable. God is the source of life. Although the Declaration doesn't specifically mention Jesus Christ, through Him everyone has access to this life.

- The task of government is to serve God.

- God is the supreme judge; we call upon him to free us from tyrants.

- As a Christian nation, we trust in God.

Many American Presidents were well aware that they depend on God, and they couldn't run the country without Him:

"It is impossible to govern the universe without the aid of a Supreme Being." (attributed to George Washington by J.K. Paulding, 1835).

"Freedom prospers when religion is vibrant and the rule of law under God acknowledged." (Ronald Reagan, 1983)

"We are never defeated unless we give up on God."(Ronald Reagan)

"And without God, democracy will not and cannot long endure. If we ever forget that we're one nation under God, then we will be a nation gone under". (Ronald Reagan, 1984)

"It is the duty of all nations to acknowledge the providence of Almighty God, to obey his will, to be grateful for His benefits, and humbly to implore His protection and favor…. (George Washington, 1789)

George Washington's direct successors in office, President John Adams and President Thomas Jefferson, also put their living faith in God into practice.

In Deuteronomy 28:1 to 28:14, to paraphrase the Bible: If we listen to God and live according to His commandments, then our country and its people will be blessed. This is what happened with the U.S.: Everything flourished and developed. People were blessed, and with God's assistance, they received blessings.

So Young America became a world power, and one of the richest and most successful countries of the world. Without planning or controlling their destiny, the United States became the world leader in many industries, such as the film industry, and the electronics industry from computers to mobile phones. The country became the blessed "land of opportunity".

The U.S. doesn't have the guarantee of the blessings of God; and the last twenty years have changed the U.S. a lot. Satan has managed to blind people more and more into thinking their faith and their relationship with God is okay. Many don't even notice how they have slowly but surely moved away from God. Some legislators and members of the government have taken actions and made decisions that are not consistent with the word of God, and God cannot approve. So if people exercise their free will and choose not to live according to the word and will of God, they will bear the consequences of their decisions. ("You reap what you sow.")

God is not intrusive. He wants us all to come to him, trusting in his help, and strive to live according to His guidance. People turn less and less to God in this country, and so the Lord withdraws gradually.

As a result, His blessings, His protection, His preservation of the country is weakening, and the curse of Satan increases. This was apparent with the attack on 9/11/2001 on the World Trade Center. It wasn't the first time that the United States was attacked in the heartland from an enemy outside its borders - with disastrous consequences. More than three thousand died and countless others were injured on 9/11. In 2001, Sylvia and I had just arrived in the U.S. We were impressed at how people united as a nation after the attacks. The President called publicly for prayer and told us that only God can help. Unfortunately, this ambiance did not last long.

Another, unprecedented catastrophic event we witnessed in the U.S.A. was in September 2008. It was the biggest stock market crash in the country's history since the Great Depression.

The impact was felt on the stock markets and the worldwide economy.   The U.S. housing market is still struggling to recover from the crisis.

Despite this, more and more decisions were made against God and His word.

Current legislation grants huge agricultural corporations and their investors tax advantages, which logically discriminate against individual and small farmers. The law is silent on the production of foods with high levels of salt, fat and HFCS and the cultivation of genetically modified plants. The attentive reader can imagine the consequences for the future health of Americans.

If someone kills a pregnant woman, they are charged with two counts of Murder. If someone participates in an abortion, which is also killing, it isn't punished. What a double standard! Each year, 1.6 million babies are aborted in the U.S.; an estimated 50 million babies have been killed since the 1970s. As a result, we now have 50 million murderers in this country. The politicians who approve this are under the control of Satan; the Bible states that Satan brought death to man from the beginning. (John 8:44).

Since summer 2015, the marriage of homosexual couples is legalized in the U.S.A. The Bible says homosexuality is an abomination to God: "'If a man has sexual relations with a man as one does with a woman, both of them have done what is detestable" (Leviticus 20:13). Marriage is made for a man and a woman: "So God created mankind in his own image, in the image of God he created them; male and female he created them." God blessed them and said to them, "Be fruitful and increase in number; fill the earth and subdue it. Rule over the fish in the sea and the birds in the sky and over every living creature that moves on the ground." (Genesis 1:27-28) "Haven't you read," he replied, "that at the beginning the

Creator 'made them male and female, and said, 'For this reason a man will leave his father and mother and be united to his wife, and the two will become one flesh. So they are no longer two, but one flesh. Therefore what God has joined together, let no one separate." (Matthew 19:4-7)

This doesn't mean that we hate or fight homosexuals; the Bible tells us to love our neighbor as ourselves. However, as Christians, we cannot go against God's Word and God's will. We cannot support homosexual marriage.

The first President of the United States introduced "school prayer". Two landmark decisions changed that, with: Engel v. Vitale in 1962 & Abington School District v. Schempp in 1963 by the Supreme Court (Supreme Court, 1962 & 1963), and school prayer has been banned in public schools in the U.S. since the decisions. It appears that many people in this country want nothing more to do with God, and if they do, they have done little to change the system to allow school prayer.

God respects our choices. Even bad choices are ours to reap, which is reflected in the crime statistics. In Huntsville, the prisons are overcrowded. What are we to do? Some are considering the release of long-term prisoners five years earlier than their sentences in order to make room for new prisoners!

Another bad choice: California is the first state to legalize the use of marijuana. The use of marijuana as well as hard drugs is rapidly on the rise. There were 1,842 drug-related deaths in the year 2000. Ten years later, the number rose to 3,036 deaths. The latest illegal drug is much cheaper than heroin, and is made of gasoline and various acids, which leads to immediate addiction and slow death.

Debt and Poverty

As a result of the real estate crisis of 2008, seven to eight million homes were foreclosed upon because some homeowners could no longer afford their loan payments due to loss of jobs, and others accepted foreclosure due to loss of equity when their property values dropped far below the mortgage debt owed. The foreclosed homes were placed on the market by lenders at extremely low prices, which adversely affected the market for all. Even homeowners who were not in foreclosure but needed to sell were forced to compete with foreclosure prices.

Foreclosures and bankruptcies are two separate economic indicators. The news channels reported high rates of foreclosures in Nevada and Florida during the mortgage crisis of 2008-2010; by 2015, Florida, New Jersey, Tennessee, Maryland, Nevada, New Mexico, Ohio, Illinois, Indiana and South Carolina were the top ten states in foreclosure statistics (DiGangi, 2015).

The highest rates of bankruptcies occurred in Alabama, Georgia, Tennessee and Utah during the time period starting in 2006. Between 2006 and 2011, there were 6,807,147 --or almost seven million Americans who filed for personal bankruptcy. Bankruptcy filing peaked in 2010 with a staggering 1,536,799 number of Americans initiating personal filings. (BankruptcyAction.com, 2014). The numbers of bankruptcies exceeded the filings of prior economic downturns, such as the one million or more bankruptcies filed in 1996. (Bank Trends, 1998).

In 2009, 32 million Americans lived below the poverty line or were at risk of poverty. By 2015, an estimated 43.1 million Americans were living below the poverty line (UC Davis Center for Poverty Research, 2016).

The official unemployment rate climbed during the economic downturn, starting in January, 2008 at 5% and reached a peak in October 2009 of 10%.(Department of Labor Statistics, 2016). If you count all the job creation activities, the unemployment rate arrived at 12% or higher during this time period.

Government debt

Today, the indebtedness of the country increases at breakneck speed; the debt increases by 2.8 million U.S. dollars per minute, or 170 million dollars per hour, (National Debt of the United States, 2017) and so it goes.

Despite this dangerous situation, the Congress debates for hours about other issues when, I believe, the national debt should be the most urgent action – for every minute counts! Eventually, the national debt will affect everything else, yet it is not on the agenda. Perhaps our legislators don't have an answer?

* * *

On another topic, I read in 2013 the U.S. government decided to help the Muslim Brotherhood by giving them a $1.5-billion dollar loan. (Breitbart.com, 2013). It is the goal of the Muslim Brotherhood to destroy Israel, infiltrate and convert the United States (a close ally with Israel) as well as all of the Western world.(The Counter Jihad Report).

The Koran allows Muslims to kill all "unbelievers" or non-Muslims who do not want to convert to Islam. Jews and Christians are their targets. The strategy of the Muslim Brotherhood is to radicalize mosques in every major city in the U.S. in order to gain spiritual rule of each city and finally of the country. In an article in the Huffington Post in 2012, the results of a survey of 98% of the mosque leaders revealed: "87 percent of mosque leaders disagree that radicalism is increasing among young Muslims. Six percent agreed that it was increasing". (Kaleem, 2012). The radicalization of America is only recognized by six percent of mosque leaders, but that is enough to plant the seed.

In the year 2000 there were 1,200 mosques in the United States. By 2010, the number of mosques increased to 2,106, almost twice as many as a decade earlier.

In Germany, there are over 2,800 mosques. Entire neighborhoods are inhabited by Muslims. In 2016, new Muslim arrivals into Germany from Syria reported feeling uncomfortable with the mosques in Germany, for they found them more radical than the mosques in Syria. (Independent, 2016). Most Muslims work, pay taxes and behave inconspicuously. They are courteous and friendly – and as long as Muslims are in the minority, it is exactly the correct jihad strategy.

As it says in the word of God, the Bible, we are to honor, love and respect our neighbors as ourselves. However, we should be wise and certainly not encourage and support projects against us, as the U.S. did with the $1.5 Billion dollar loan to Egypt's Muslim Brotherhood in 2013, (Breitbart.com, 2013), plus the $400 million released to the hostile Muslim government in Iran in

January 2016 (Fortune.com, 2016).

To quote the Bible:

Jesus said to them: "Truly, truly, I say to you, before Abraham was, I am." (John 8:58)

Jesus said to him: "I am the way, the truth, and the life. No one comes to the Father except through me." (John 14:6)

"And many false prophets will arise and lead many astray."(Matthew 24:11)

Weapons and Supplies

In times of a poor economic climate, many Americans are more and more fearful. Some expect an implosion in a few years, or a total economic collapse. The day that money is worth nothing, there would be no electricity, no water, and no one could buy food or gas ... with further disastrous consequences. After a few days, looting would start.

The fears are good news for weapons manufacturers. Many Americans are buying several weapons and ammunition to defend themselves and their families. A friend told me that he had hidden loaded firearms throughout the house: on each floor and in all the main rooms. He wanted to have them immediately at hand in an emergency.

Other friends are preparing in different ways, and have purchased small water treatment systems in order to produce drinking water from the nearby Tennessee

River. They also have a thousand-liter gas tank to store fuel for the car and a small generator. The generator produces enough electricity to operate their refrigerators, their heating and air conditioning, their computers, and can charge their mobile phones. They also stocked food: flour, oil, canned meat, milk powder and other perishable items.

One Nation Under God?

Americans are a religious people: Each year between 1990 and 2000, an average of 1,000 new churches were founded. Unfortunately, more churches close their doors forever – over 4,000 closings a year. This means there are three thousand fewer churches in the country with each passing year. (Krejcir, 2007). According to official figures in the United States between 1992 and 2002, 77% to 87% or 160 million of Americans in 2002 identified themselves as Christians (Krejcir, 2007). Out of 314 million inhabitants in the U.S., the remaining 154 million are of other faiths, or are non-religious. Considering the population, this places the U.S. as the #4 country worldwide as ripe for Missionary work within its own borders.

The divorce rate in this country is approximately 50%; in Huntsville, Alabama, 13.7% have been divorced at least once (Jennifer, 2016). Alabama is second only to Alaska in the divorce rate in the U.S. (InsideGov.com, 2017). God does not want any human being to get a divorce once married. In Huntsville, there are over 100 churches, and they appear full every Sunday. Is it possible that over 50% of churchgoers' marriages end in divorce also?

Once I invited Jesus into my life, I made Him master of my life. Since then, He lives in me through His Holy Spirit. My life changes slowly and steadily to the better. I will do the things in life as Jesus would. My faith helps my marriage, so there is not much room for sin.

How does Faith fit with divorces among Christians? I believe that many no longer walk with God. Perhaps divorced churchgoers had no personal relationship with God at the time of their divorce. Some may just go to church because their parents and the grandparents did so. Attending church is just a tradition, and even that tradition is declining in the U.S. In 1992, 22% of Americans frequently attended church. By 2002, only 18% frequently attended church. (Krejcir, 2007). Soon, the U.S. will catch up with Europe's 8% in church attendance! It seems that churchgoers attend not to meet with God, but to meet with other people! During services, Christians probably hear the word of God, but they do not act on it, because Jesus does not live within them. They are "Checklist-Christians": On Sunday, the church service is on the "to-do" list, so they go, then it is done, so it can be deleted from the checklist.

Attending church doesn't make someone automatically a Christian. The root of "Christian" is Christ. Anyone who believes that they are a **Christian** simply because they goes to **church** is mistaken. For example: You do not become a car because you are in the **garage**.

Money Reigns the World - and Increasingly the Churches?

Many non-believers say, "I don't want to have anything

to do with 'Christians' because they talk holy but act exactly the opposite." A waitress who served us in a restaurant once told us if she works Sundays and sees a table where people pray before meals, she would rather not wait on that table. She stated that people who pray before meals demanded the most of her, and tipped her the least. So, how does that work with "prosperity gospel," which plays a major role in the U.S.? Many Christians believe that their financial wealth and well-being are the will of God, so donations to charity increase their success. Maybe it doesn't work at all?

There are churches in the U.S. with up to 40,000 worshipers *per service*. These events are broadcast live on television to reach many more people. In our early years in the U.S., I listened to sermons from these "mega-churches" and was thrilled: The Pastor always had a clear, encouraging, and inspiring message, without slip-ups in his speech. Very often the subject of the sermon pertained to the many blessings of God – that blessings could be seen on financial, health and professional success. Everything you do, or start to do, would be a success with God's help. And who doesn't want that?

It took me a while before I realized: Biblically, these are only half-truths. The bottom line was that the Pastor's preaching was exactly what I, and others wanted to hear, and it made everybody feel very good. Afterwards, the audience was so excited, they could hardly wait for the next service! I think it is the nature of each human being that we feel at ease when we hear a positive, promising message. Many pastors have understood that principal and taken it to heart, which explains the high number of attendees in their churches. However, the Bible warns us: "Watch out for false prophets. They come to you in sheep's clothing, but inwardly they are ferocious wolves." (Matthew 7:15)

"See to it that no one takes you captive through hollow and deceptive philosophy, which depends on human tradition and the elemental spiritual forces of this world rather than on Christ." (Colossians 2:8)

"Let no one deceive you with empty words, for because of such things God's wrath comes on those who are disobedient." (Ephesians 5:6)

Jesus answered: "Watch out that no one deceives you." (Matthew 24:4)

These same pastors preach the law of "you reap what you sow": "Do not be deceived: God cannot be mocked. A man reaps what he sows." (Galatians 6:7). Whoever gives plenty will also reap bountifully. According to the Bible, one should give, as Abraham gave, a tenth of his income to the kingdom of God, which means to the church and to the needy. "When you have finished setting aside a tenth of all your produce in the third year, the year of the tithe, you shall give it to the Levite, the foreigner, the fatherless and the widow, so that they may eat in your towns and be satisfied." (Deuteronomy 26:12).

Those who fail to do so would reap nothing-- that is, they would not be blessed financially. If someone earned three thousand dollars a month, they should give three hundred dollars a month as tithe. I once did the math: if 20,000 people attend a church service and the preacher encourages people to give, lets say $50, the income for the service would be a million dollars!

It is God's law: "sowing and reaping" is a message from the Bible, so it is a spiritual truth; Paul writes more than once about it. However, we should not give what *the pastor* tells us - nor what other people tell us, nor the calculator. We should pray and ask *the Lord* what amount is right for us. If we have a fixed monthly income, we can schedule a fixed monthly amount for the kingdom of God.

How much we should give will determine our "inner peace", if we have inner peace about a specific amount, then this is the amount we should give. The amount may be even more than ten percent.

Back to the Mega-feel-good churches: Unfortunately, the Gospel of the Bible, which is what Jesus really preached, is mostly embezzled. At the mega-churches, one does not hear a lot of sermons on Bible verses such as: " Then Jesus said to his disciples, "Whoever wants to be my disciple must deny themselves and take up their cross and follow me."(Matthew 16:24). Also: "Going a little farther, he fell with his face to the ground and prayed, "My Father, if it is possible, may this cup be taken from me. Yet not as I will, but as you will." (Matthew 26:39)

Not many sermons mention what the Apostle Paul experienced in his service for Jesus: : "Five times I received from the Jews thirty-nine lashes. Three times I was beaten with rods, once I was stoned, three times I was shipwrecked, a night and a day I have spent in the deep. I have been on frequent journeys, in dangers from rivers, dangers from robbers, dangers from my countrymen, dangers from the Gentiles, dangers in the city, dangers in the wilderness, dangers on the sea, dangers among false brethren; I have been in labor and hardship, through many sleepless nights, in hunger and thirst, often without food, in cold and exposure. Apart from such external things, there is the daily pressure on me of concern for all the churches. Who is weak without my being weak? Who is led into sin without my intense concern? If I have to boast, I will boast of what pertains to my weakness. The God and Father of the Lord Jesus, He who is blessed forever, knows that I am not lying." (2 Corinthians 11:24-31).

This is not to say, if we believe in God, we would have to suffer. No! If we believe in Jesus Christ, and when we believe that He has paid on the cross for all of our sins, then most important of all, we have the promise of eternal life. We can be together in eternity with Him, where there is no disease, no worries and hardships; neither strife and hatred, nor greed; and we can look forward to eternal life.

But as the cited Bible verses illustrate: Living with Jesus doesn't mean we always walk in sunshine; sometimes He permits us to walk through dark valleys in order to form us for what is to come. But even then, Jesus is always with us. He loves us and He never lets us down.

It is argued, of the 314 million residents of the United States, 154 million are either non-believers in any religion or are non-Christians practicing another faith. Accordingly, 160 million are Christians. Imagine if 160 million Americans decided to pray for their country, and asked God for solutions to the problems that I have already enumerated - surely God would intervene. With His intervention, and a lot of issues could be resolved in this country. Therefore, I can only surmise that a small percentage of Americans have a personal relationship with God.

I asked my son, "How many of your friends probably believe in God?" His answer was: "None! Many justify their disbelief with the hardship and the suffering in this world and ask how a loving, all-powerful God could allow that." Well, consider this example: A hairdresser tells the customer: "There is no God. If there is a God, then why people do get sick and die too early? Why is there so much injustice in the world, with all the wars and hunger? If God is love, how can He allow all this?" The customer doesn't reply, and changes the subject. Upon leaving the barber shop, the customer sees a beggar sitting on the sidewalk with long, greasy, unkempt hair, so he turns around and goes back to the hairdresser and declares: "There is no hairdresser in this world." The hairdresser replies: "What do you mean?!" The customer answers: "Well, if there were a hairdresser, how could any hairdresser allow people to look like the beggar in front of your shop!" The hairdresser thinks carefully and says: "The beggar never came to me to cut his hair!"

God gave us free will, and He respects it: When we invite God, He is there, and if not, then He will stay away.

14 From 100 to 0 in 1 Second, Part Three

Our three sons inherited the love of motorcycles, or did they learn to love motorcycles from me? Anyway, each of them had a motorcycle license, and once a year we took a motorcycle trip. We rented the motorcycles and usually spent one night in a nice cabin somewhere in the Smokey Mountains. The winding roads on the way to the Smokey Mountains are a treat for motorcyclists. In 2012, as usual, we rented a comfortable cabin for our stay. The "cabins" come in all sizes, and usually they are very beautiful, located in the woods or on a small hill with idyllic views. One can barbecue on the balconies or behind the houses, and enjoy the beautiful evenings. The rooms are pleasantly rustic, and one immediately feels comfortable and "at home". Therefore, we decided to arrive at the cabin by early afternoon, because we wanted to enjoy the comfort and the nice views from the cabin.

Our trip in Autumn 2012 was no different. Patrick had his own motorcycle; Gilbert, Kevin and I always borrowed one at the Harley-Davidson dealership. As with every year, I called my insurance agent to make certain the rental bike would be insured, and the clerk confirmed that since I have insurance for the car, the rental bike will be automatically insured. I thanked her explicitly for the quick and positive response. Just before our trip, Gilbert received the offer to go to Nashville to see the filming of a famous television series. He did not want to miss the opportunity, so he canceled the motorcycle trip.

The next day, I started the day as I had for 18 years, with my personal prayer time, and then Sylvia and I prayed together. On that morning, as we always did before such trips, we prayed specifically for God's guidance and protection for all of us. Then, we were ready for departure.

* * *

The best thing about motorcycling is the curves — for we enjoy braking and then accelerating. The long straight roads where one could reach maximum speeds didn't interest us as much. With the speed limits in the U.S., a nice straight highway would be boring and rather frustrating! So we planned the route carefully, to enjoy lots of curves. On the edge of Huntsville, we went over a small mountain range and drove three kilometers along the ridge in beautiful weather. Kevin went ahead, I was in the middle, and Patrick was behind us.

Each trail came to an end, and then it went downhill. The drive was just as we desired, with beautiful curves, and was a real pleasure for us! On the other side of the mountain, the road was still in shadow. To this day, I still don't know for sure if the shadow was the reason, but I drove off the road after the second curve.

The ground sloped steeply to the right of the road, and I crashed into the nearest tree. I wasn't driving very fast, perhaps 25 miles per hour, but I hit the tree with my helmet, my shoulder, and my chest. I was immediately unconscious. Kevin had seen nothing of the accident because he was in front of me. After 2 miles, he realized that we were no longer behind him. Patrick saw everything because he was right behind me, without being able to do anything about it. It was the worst

104

experience for him.

I have a very good relationship with my three sons, I love them and they love me. So I can imagine how bad it must have been for Patrick and Kevin to see me down the steep slope, motionless against the tree. Patrick immediately called the ambulance. They were alone with me. The problem was that the motorcycle was lying on top of me. Due to gravity, there was a chance the bike could slide and crush me. After all, the weight of the bike was well over half a ton. Patrick and Kevin desperately tried to pull the Harley away from me, but they did not succeed, not even with the help of another person who arrived at scene. For Kevin and Patrick, it was one of the worst experiences of their lives.

* * *

Within minutes after Patrick's 911 Emergency call, the fire department arrived and administered first aid. With the fire station closer to the accident, they were first responders on the scene. Firefighters are trained and competent rescuers. Then, the ambulance arrived and I was taken to the nearest hospital with lights flashing and sirens. I was still unconscious.

Patrick followed the ambulance, and Kevin stayed at the accident scene to answer questions from the police and to wait for the tow truck.

After answering the questions of the police, Kevin called Sylvia and explained to her what had happened. Sylvia asked about my condition. Kevin told her that I was still breathing, so I was probably still alive. Patrick's wife had to work that Saturday, so their children were with Sylvia. When the children saw Sylvia crying, they wanted to know what had happened! Sylvia told them about the accident and then all three were crying. They also started to pray for me, asking God to take me into His hands and begged that everything turn out well.

My wife then called Gilbert. Gilbert had returned from Nashville in the middle of the night and wanted to sleep in. As he told me later, he suddenly woke up with the feeling that something was wrong, and could not fall asleep again! It became clear to him upon hearing the news of my accident that he had awakened exactly at the time of the accident.

Sylvia took the children to Gilbert, and his wife took care of them. Then Sylvia and Gilbert drove to the hospital, where Kevin and Patrick were in the waiting area at the emergency room. Later, both daughters-in-law arrived with the children at the emergency room. Before I was transferred to the intensive care unit, Sylvia and my three sons were allowed to see me. The children's access to see me in the emergency room was denied. I floated in and out of consciousness, and was unable to perceive anything.

* * *

The diagnosis for my condition was: seven broken ribs, a punctured lung, a pelvic rupture and a severe brain trauma. It all sounded very worrying. The doctor told my family that the brain injury was very critical, and if the bleeding didn't stop shortly, they would have to operate.

The situation made it very difficult for everyone. Patrick's face was almost white and he behaved abnormally - he was in shock. Sylvia saw Patrick's condition first, and immediately asked the doctors if they could help him.

However, no one responded to Sylvia's request... and Patrick's shock continued for three more days.

Kevin processed it quite differently. He was the only son still living at home, so he said to himself: "I must be strong now; I must help my mother and be on her side". His emotional trauma showed up only a few months later, in extreme situations, indicating how much the horror of the accident still shook him. Gilbert was able to handle it best, for he had not witnessed the accident nor seen me on the side of the tree.

On the day of the accident, my wife informed my relatives and friends. She asked them to pray for me - and by the next morning, the brain bleeding had stopped and surgery wasn't necessary! Even with the good news, I still had serious issues. The punctured lung caused breathing problems for me, so an oxygen mask was set up. Through a small cut on the belly, a tube was inserted into the lungs so the fluid could drain. I was fed intravenously.

* * *

During moments of consciousness, I wondered what all the tubing and cables in my body were, as well as the machines and equipment around me. Sylvia, my sons and my daughters-in-law knew, but I had a memory like a baby. No matter what they told me, after two minutes I had forgotten everything, and I asked again - and again ... until I grew tired, babbled and finally fell asleep.

The rib fractures and the broken pelvis were not treated at first. As for my memory loss, Gilbert found a brilliant solution: he hung an "info poster" with the important information on what had happened in front of me on the wall. So, I was always up to date and didn't have to ask questions every two minutes. That helped everyone.

In the intensive care unit, the visits were strictly regulated: three people were allowed to stay with me three times a day for twenty minutes. During these short visits and with my serious brain condition, I was convinced that the doctors had simply put me in I.C.U. without my consent, and I protested. I told my wife in all seriousness that I wanted to get out every time I saw her.

I still couldn't think clearly. During one visit, Kevin and Sylvia had already said good-bye, and I pulled out all the tubing in an unguarded moment and got out of bed. (Without all the pain medicine, I probably would not have done it. I was feeling no pain so it didn't hurt to move.) Luckily, Kevin looked over his shoulder on his way out and saw me walking across the hospital floor. He ran back to me, calmed me down, and got me back to bed. On one occasion, I had to be tied down, for I absolutely wanted to get away from there.

Slowly, my overall condition improved. I no longer needed a respiratory mask, the lung drainage tube was removed, and my memory had become somewhat improved. I still didn't want to be in the intensive care unit and wanted to get out of the hospital!

* * *

I must have been quite an annoyance to the doctors. In any case, they decided I should leave the intensive care unit - on one condition: my relatives would have to look after me around the clock, because my memory was still very incomplete.

Sylvia made a schedule per the doctors' request and to make me happy, so I was transferred to a regular hospital room seven days after the accident. My entire family helped meet the schedule: Kevin was able to adapt his study plans to sit with me by day, and my sister-in-law spent her long lunch breaks with me. My wife stayed with me at night, where she slept on a chair.

Everyone did their very best to ensure 24-hour care. Unbelievably, only five days later, I was allowed to leave the hospital with a walking aid. It wasn't long afterward that I learned that such brain injuries (similar to those of Michael Schumacher) were fatal in most cases. God Hears Prayer!

Sylvia had to carry the largest burden; not only did she deal with the life-threatening condition in which I hovered, she also endured the uncertainty, and provided the round-the-clock care. In addition, the company also depended on Sylvia. At the time of the accident, Werner was with his wife, Monika on a business trip in Germany, and I was the second man in charge after Werner. My brother cut short his stay in Germany. However, Sylvia and Werner's son, Timo had to cover a few days on their own until Werner arrived back in the States. The situation burdened Sylvia greatly.

When I consider what my family did for me during this time ---especially my wife, but also my sons and their families – (Patrick and his wife Jay, and their sons Alexander and Carlos; Gilbert and his wife Michelle, as well as our youngest son, Kevin)– I can't thank them enough. The children stood with their mother like a rock, and, of course, with me.

My first days at home were particularly challenging. I had

to rely on help for everything: getting dressed, taking a shower, shaving, eating, walking, and climbing stairs. It was quite a few days before I could take the first small steps with the walker by myself. My memory also improved slowly.

The doctors recommended speech therapy for me, and I regularly had physiotherapy. I could not drive, so the "Taxi Sylvia" was commenced! All my therapies had to be juggled into the schedule because Sylvia still had her job and responsibilities at the company. All the employees, and especially my brother and his wife gave us 100% support.

* * *

In the USA, things are much different than in Germany, not just with food. If you have a good employer, you get paid two weeks holidays in the United States. I used up my 2 weeks for my hospital stay. In any other company, I wouldn't have received additional payment, so I am very grateful to Werner for continuing to pay my salary.

Back then, there was no law requiring people to have health insurance. However, Sylvia and I had health insurance, with a $10,000 deductible per year. The high deductible allowed us to lower the monthly payments. The high deductible also meant we had to pay the first $10,000 out of our pockets. The total cost for my hospitalization was over $100,000. Since therapy and treatments continued into the following year, we had to pay a total of $20,000 for the deductible, which was reset every January 1st.

We had rented the Harley-Davidson. One week before our departure, we were assured the motorcycle would

110

be covered by my car insurance. I was shocked to learn from the rental agency that my insurance company wouldn't cover the damage to the motorcycle! The damages amounted to $5,300!

Of course, I immediately contacted my insurance company. To my great surprise, I was told it was not covered and they couldn't imagine who in their office could have made such a statement! I informed them that my wife had listened to the conversation where they assured me it was covered, but it was pointless to argue with the insurance company. So we had to pay the $5300.

All in all, the accident cost us in excess of $25,000. I was unable to work, so at least Sylvia had her work. The speech therapist arrived at a point that she felt she had done everything that was possible, and she could no longer help me. The best brain training would be if I resumed my work.

* * *

Although I slept a lot after my hospital stay, the pain awoke me three or four times per night. I moved from the bed to the couch and back to the bed again. Despite physiotherapy, I was very limited with my right arm, and could only lift my arm up to shoulder height. Despite all this, I decided to return to work four weeks after the accident.

Returning to work was not easy. As a general manager, one bears the overall responsibility for the business, and one has to settle everything that is not going well. The ease I had in the job before the accident was gone, and even minor problems became insurmountable. Every morning, I asked God for guidance and help, but everything was so difficult. Finally, the staff told me I was no longer the same since the accident. Four months after the accident, I was totally exhausted and at the end of my tether. Surely this was mainly due to my brain injury, but also due to missing sleep at night.

My wife was physically and mentally at the end of her strength, perhaps even more than I. The accident and its consequences had demanded too much. After much thought, prayer and consultation with Werner, we decided to take a "time out" for two months. After that, we both hoped to come back fully operational and fully recovered.

During this time, I also wanted to get surgery on my shoulder. The doctors had found that the muscle-tendon cap was torn, and assured me that surgery could completely solve the problem. I let them do the surgery right at the beginning of our time out and started physiotherapy right away. After four weeks, I was able to use my right arm again in full range.

* * *

Everything in my life changed and was upside down within a single second. I had been living my life with an average speed of 100 and without warning, it changed to zero within one second.

My life could have been finished, and only with God's protection and plan, my life was not quite finished. Patrick discovered that "my" tree was hollow. Ironically, the one tree in which I had crashed with full force was hollow? I couldn't believe it, and I had to see it for myself! The scene of the accident was only a few miles

112

away so we went there. Indeed, the force of my impact had knocked a hole in the bottom of the tree.

The tree was about four stories tall and the trunk had a diameter of 45 inches. A tree of this size usually does not yield or move at all on impact, which is the reason many motorcyclists are killed when they hit a tree. Just "my" tree was hollow on the inside! How could that be? The tree stood at exactly the right place – for without the tree, I would have tumbled down the steep, rocky slope and died in the fall. If the tree had been as solid as the other trees, I wouldn't have survived the impact.

I knew God could have prevented the accident, especially since we had prayed for God's protection a few hours earlier. I am also aware that the Lord had delivered a miracle in spite of the accident, because of that special tree. Why God allowed this to happen, I do not have an answer. Some of it I can understand, and it seems that God has something else planned for me on this earth. Why else would he have protected my life in such a wonderful way?

15 The Year "After"

My shoulder had healed, and the second month of our "time out" felt relaxing. Our time out was coming to an end, and I did not feel that I could or should go back to work at that point. My memory was still very unreliable. So we invited Werner and Monika over for a dinner and a talk.

Frankly, I did not dare say that I still wanted to wait; I asked my brother if he needed both of us back. They said they could handle the business if I stayed out a little longer, but they needed Sylvia since she handled the bookkeeping and a lot more. Her being off had been anything but easy for the company, and they wanted my wife back sooner rather than later.

Werner and his son, Timo took over my job of running the company. Timo had been in the company for over 15 years, and is slated be the future President of the company. The company didn't have as many jobs, so they could cope with my tasks without a problem. The timing was right and the company saved some money. When I heard they could handle things for a while longer, it was a great relief to me. I could go forward slowly, step by step.

Werner offered instead for me to work in the field and sell whatever the company had to offer which would boost its sales. As always in such situations, I said I would pray about it and ask the Lord what He had planned for me next.

A few days later Sylvia went back to accounting, and I

was home - with plenty of time to pray and read the Bible, to talk with the Lord and to think.

* * *

A few months after we moved to Huntsville, I gained weight. To lose weight and for exercise, I started to jog in the morning, (before my accident in 2012). At first I ran for two miles; over time I reached five miles. When I heard about the "Country Music Marathon Nashville" - and that one could also run half a marathon - I considered it. I had already mastered five miles a day, and there were ten weeks to increase my mileage to 13 miles. I felt that it was possible, so I registered for Nashville.

It takes two hours to get to Nashville, the capital of country music. The race would run through the city, where every two miles a live band would play alongside the marathon route in order to keep the runners motivated. It sounded really good!

I had 10 weeks left before the race and put together a training plan. The plan showed that I should run at least 30 miles a week, and two weeks before the race, I should reach my highest mileage per day which suggested should be around 12 miles per day. The mileage should then be reduced with no running at all in the last 4 days before the race. I adamantly tried sticking to the training plan, but it was increasingly stressful and time consuming. It had a good side: While running, I had plenty of time to pray and talk to God about everything.

On the day before the big race, Sylvia and I went to Nashville and stayed at a hotel right next to the starting line. That was perfect because there were over 20,000 runners registered– which I did not know. The run started at seven a.m. It would have taken hours to get to the starting line, but I was able to walk there from our hotel. In front of me were ten thousand runners, and ten thousand behind me. They all had the same goal: Everyone wanted to reach to finish line in the best possible time. It felt like a secret society to be with the runners. We had great conversations. The entire experience was incredibly impressive and unforgettable.

A live band played at the starting line, and two miles down the road was the next live band. It was inspiring. Unfortunately for me, it was too inspiring. Due to my inexperience, I set a pace that was way too fast in the beginning, and after five miles my enthusiasm changed to disillusionment.

At "mile marker eight", I was completely exhausted and thoughts ran through my head, such as: "You will never reach the finish line, you have no breath anymore; you're much too weak, give it up!" Out of desperation, I began to pray at some point, "Lord, You tell us in Your word: Ask me and it will be given to you. That is why I now ask You: Help me! I am finished, I am done. I want to give up, only with Your help will I be able to do it. "

A few seconds after the prayer, another runner passed me with a Bible verse on the back of his shirt: "Jesus says: Everything is possible for one who believes" (Mark 9:23). The man was in front of me for a few minutes, with the Bible verse in view, and then he disappeared into the mass of the other runners. That was God's answer to my prayer! So I kept running.

At "mile marker 11", I was again about to give up –but I was passed by another runner with exactly the same

Bible verse on his back! So, I reached the finish line two hours later with the very last of my strength, and only through God's powerful help. On the spot, I swore to myself: "I'll never do this again! Never ever!"

Since then, I've been to the Nashville marathon three times as a runner, and participated in many other shorter races. These endurance races led me back to my limits; so the Lord showed me that there are no limits for Him and that only He can make the impossible possible.

Seven months after the accident and just a few weeks after the end of our "time out" came the right motivation to get my body back in shape. Since I was not a novice in running, I made up my mind to join a 10K run in Huntsville.

The race went very well; after an hour and three minutes, I ran across the finish line - given the injuries, that was a good performance! Today, as I write this, is the thirtieth day after Michael Schumacher's skiing accident. I wish him speedy recovery and I pray that he can recover as well as I did, especially with his serious head injury.

* * *

Since I was a stay-at-home-husband, the perk of a company car ended. We managed with one car. Sylvia drove our car to work and I got it when needed by dropping her off at work and picking her up in the evening. In warm weather, I used the bicycle, which was also good exercise.

I felt isolated as if God had put me on a deserted island. For a whole year, I had almost no contact or conversation with anyone outside of my family members. Surprisingly, I could live with it.

Much worse for me, as the former manager, was that I wasn't able to manage my life since I didn't know in which direction I was to go. I prayed a lot more than before, yet I had no idea what God wanted me to do and in which direction He would lead me.

In such a situation, many people might despair or depart from the Faith. Although I often wasn't doing well, I knew by God's grace that He was always with me. There was nothing there anymore of my old life, yet God had everything under control. This strengthened my relationship, my trust in the Lord; I never doubted Him at this time.

It was clear: Sooner or later we would use up all of our savings. Would God allow us once again to lose everything and have nothing? We had already experienced a total loss of funds in which we didn't even have money to buy something to eat. Would that be the case again?

* * *

In September 2013, my work visa expired and there was no way to extend it. From October on, I would no longer be allowed to work in the country. Even if I had found a job, I would not be able to work without a work permit. I did not even know what to seek as work. Normally God puts a desire into our hearts, showing us the direction in which to proceed.

For me, there was only emptiness. So I really arrived at zero: $ 25,000 in debt, no job, no car, no future, unable to work in the country, soon insolvent and facing a looming foreclosure...

During this time, God showed me what really matters in life. Our life expectancy is currently at about 75 years. The Bible says that after death, not everything is over; it is the reverse. Life only begins when we start Eternity and we spend it either with God or with the devil.

What does God offer us? Love, peace, joy, gentleness, patience, beauty and glory in abundance, but no disease, no pain, no need, no poverty. How is it, however, in the kingdom of the devil? It is: hatred, strife, war, lies, deceit, deception, hatred, poverty, suffering, distress, disease – and all forever and ever.

In order to understand Eternity a little bit better, here is a comparison: On Earth, we spend about 75 years. Suppose eternity lasted 5000 years, our time on Earth would be 1.5% of Eternity.

To understand it even better: God not only created the Earth, but the entire universe, which everybody knows is eternal. It takes light approximately 30,000 light years to get to the center of our galaxy. The moon is 380,000 kilometers away, and with the speed of light, light would travel to the moon in 1.2 seconds.

This example gives an idea of how great and powerful God must be. I know one thing: I want to do everything in my power to spend the future, my eternity, with the Creator of the universe; with God. Don't you think that should be the most important goal for everyone?

If God is in charge of our life, He promises in His Word: "Therefore I tell you, do not worry about your life, what you will eat or drink; or about your body, what you will wear. Is not life more than food, and the body more than clothes? Look at the birds of the air; they do not sow or reap or store away in barns, and yet your heavenly Father feeds them. Are you not much more valuable than they? Can any one of you by worrying add a single hour to your life?"

"And why do you worry about clothes? See how the flowers of the field grow. They do not labor or spin. Yet I tell you that not even Solomon in all his splendor was dressed like one of these. If that is how God clothes the grass of the field, which is here today and tomorrow is thrown into the fire, will he not much more clothe you— you of little faith? So do not worry, saying, 'What shall we eat?' or 'What shall we drink?' or 'What shall we wear?' For the pagans run after all these things, and your heavenly Father knows that you need them. But seek first his kingdom and his righteousness, and all these things will be given to you as well. Therefore do not worry about tomorrow, for tomorrow will worry about itself. Each day has enough trouble of its own." (Matthew 6:25-34).

It is precisely what we had experienced in Germany and we were never disappointed. On the contrary, sometimes He gave us even more than we expected or needed. So I knew He wouldn't let us down in this situation.

* * *

I thought about my twelve years in the U.S. and wondered: Was the Lord really most important for me, as it is written in the first commandment? Or in time, did other things become more important than God?

120

I realized that the devil worked slowly but steadily and that little things of everyday life became so important to me that I was missing something when I had to give it up.

For example, watching TV as soon as I came home in the evening, or drinking 1-2 glass of wine after dinner... I am grateful that the Lord has shown in His grace my "little gods"!

These things seem small and insignificant, but for God nothing is too little. He cannot tolerate impurity. When Moses encountered God on Mount Horeb, God said: "you cannot see my face, for no one may see me and live." (Exodus 33:20) For all the people laden with sin, God's presence would have been certain death for them. "For the wages of sin is death, but the gift of God is eternal life in Christ Jesus our Lord" (Romans 6:23). The Bible says that we have to be without sin, if we want to get closer to the Lord.

Therefore, Jesus suffered on the cross for us, in order take on all sins of the world. This act opened a door to God and to Heaven for all human beings.

How great and mighty, powerful, holy, and full of love is our God! And no matter how small, He knows exactly how many hairs we have on our heads. He knows me inside and out, He can see into my heart and He knows my thoughts. Time is not a limitation for Him; time does not exist. There is no past, present, nor future. He already knows what I'll do tomorrow. Therefore, I tell Him everything and that is how I want to live, praying:

"Lord, You have the best plan for my life. Your Word says that You have only good things in mind for me. Therefore, no more should be done by my will but Yours.

Even though I do not understand sometimes why things get so out of hand, and I do not succeed, and develop differently than I have imagined or planned - I want to trust You wholeheartedly with all I have. The path that You have for me is perfect and great, and the path that is Your path is where I want to go."

* * *

The prayer changed how I looked at my serious accident of 2012 and the huge problems that followed, being the huge debt that I had, no work, no car, and the threat of insolvency with foreclosure. I realized that even if God allowed us to lose the house and everything else – then this would also be part of His perfect plan. He has everything under control!

There would have been no problem for God to prevent the accident, especially since we had specifically prayed in the morning for God's protection and preservation. I trust Him, that He has good reasons for it! Some of it I can already see, because God has shown his greatness in the mighty miracles of the hollow tree that saved my life. The Bible says: "And we know that in all things God works for the good of those who love him, who have been called according to his purpose" (Romans 8:28). I believe the accident will turn out for the better in my life, even if I cannot see right now how this could be accomplished.

Some things I can already see have changed for the better:

• I have much more time for the Lord, for prayer, and for conversation with him.

- God once again became the center of my life, as it says in the first commandment: There are no other gods except Him. He is most important in my life and in 1st place.

- God has placed in my heart to pray constantly: for our city here, for the state and for this country, for all the countries in the world, especially for Germany and the United States, and my family, my relatives and friends both far and near; that all people who do not know God, experience His grace and love and that God touches their hearts. May He give them a desire to come to Him and to entrust their lives to Him through Jesus Christ.

- I realized that only God is able to open the human heart; only He can make them willing to draw nearer to Him. When I speak to someone about God and his heart and mind is not open, I could talk for hours and it would still do nothing. Whom the Lord touches, he will experience God's grace. So I pray to God that He reaches the hearts and minds of everyone who reads this book.

- Before the accident, I might have prayed an hour a day; now I pray a lot longer. In Germany I have worshiped God often with singing and playing songs on the keyboard. In the years before my accident, that was completely gone, but now I have begun again.

- God gave me the time to write this book. My most important goal is not for my own praise but for God to receive all the glory, honor, and praise; and, through reading this book, people will start a new life with Jesus.

- God gave me more time to read His Word in the Bible and through it, He spoke in a special way to me.

- God has shown me how really dark it is in this world and how much we need Him and His grace, kindness and mercy. Before my accident, I thought everything seemed to be ok, except for some small issues in this country and in the world. I had no time to get detailed information and to recognize reality.

- Only now I understand: If Jesus came today, billions of people would go to Hell instead to Heaven and it would be for Eternity. Jesus made it so simple for us: He gives us free tickets for Heaven. It does not cost us anything; it cost Him everything. We only need to say yes to Jesus.

- God showed me: There are over 100 Churches in Huntsville and they are full every Sunday, but there are still not a lot Christians who really follow Jesus according to the Commandments. Therefore, we urgently need revival, even in the "Christian camp".

- God taught me to appreciate much more of what my wife does. Before my accident, she ran the household - she cooked and cleaned the house, took care of the laundry and more, and all this in addition to her job as the bookkeeper in the company.

- God has shown me that I can get along well on my "desert island", where I have only Him and my family, without contact with the outside world. Often, I talk with no one all day from eight to five, and when Sylvia comes home, she's my only interlocutor.

- I am not saying that we should isolate ourselves; I just want to say that everything is possible with God. People who have no relationship with God would probably be lost.

Creating this list has encouraged me and showed me how much God has used the accident to change me for the better!

* * *

My relationship with God – my friendship with God the Father, Jesus and the Holy Spirit - guarantees blessings, wisdom, peace, effective work, love, justice, security, stability, strength, joy, and success. I am so happy for it! I have no idea how I lived and handled life without Jesus, when I lived my life as if other things were more important than Him.

Let's imagine a situation in which your boss knows for certain that selling a particular product would bring huge success to you, to the company, and to all employees. Shouldn't you and everyone else in the company concentrate on that? Wouldn't it be fatal to concentrate on something else? Likewise, I see the connection with the Lord: It would be disastrous if we didn't concentrate on Him, for we would miss all the blessings as promised in the Bible.

So to conclude this chapter, I re-emphasize that we should give the highest priority to our relationship with God. We shouldn't neglect Him, but we should put Him in first place. Then the blessings will follow that God has promised us. Don't we want that?

16 The Mission

My time in the United States has been very educational for me, especially the year after my serious accident. I learned many new things, and I learned to see familiar things with new eyes. I want to summarize what is most important for me, and then I will show what the solution might be.

In relation to the total population in the United States, there are a few people in the business world who have tremendous power and an enormous amount of money. These few people use their power and large capital recklessly to their advantage in order to gain more power and capital. They are masters of deceiving the people of the United States and the world.

Life-threatening Illusion: Death in the Pot

In his book "How Do You Kill 11 Million People?" Andy Andrews describes how eleven million people were killed, including six million Jews between 1933 and 1945 through lies and deception. (Hyatt, 2012).

It appears that the current government as of 2015 and the media in the U.S. are trying to do exactly the same: each individual is mediated in this country. We are led to believe that, other than a few small issues, everything is running smoothly and is okay - but those are lies and deceptions.

The list of lies and deceptions is long – everything from

unhealthy food, harmful meat and dairy products, additives to food and drink that are harmful to the body, hormones and antibiotics injected into cattle, fish, poultry, and other meat sources, and toxins used in our fields are slowly killing 310 million Americans.

GMO soya and corn grown in millions of square miles, are resistant to weed killer. The large fields are sprayed from the air; the weed dies, the crop continues to grow. This type of farming is a lot cheaper than the traditional method. Farmers who use natural seeds have difficulty to stay in business because they are barely competitive. In my opinion, the genetically modified products are harmful to a large extent, and the healthy nutrients originally created by God are missing.

The manufacturer adds small amounts of substances to the food to create consumer addiction. In order to make the food look nice and attract consumers, dyes are mixed into foods, which also have devastating effects on health.

In my opinion, this is deliberate poisoning; the consequences as of this date are:

- At least two-thirds of US citizens are overweight, of which one third is obese.

- One third of the children are overweight or obese. If the trend continues, 43% of all Americans will be obese in ten years! After smoking, obesity is the second leading cause of premature death (cardiovascular diseases, diabetes).

- 41% of all Americans living today are likely to get cancer in their lifetimes, with more people getting cancer every second!

128

Gloomy prospects

To summarize the economic and social situation in the country, almost no one wants to have anything to do with God, and many want to govern the country without God. The impact is that the United States is in great distress.

The national debt is rising by $4 billion dollars a day, and is now around 35% higher than that of Greece. Over 8 million homes have been foreclosed upon and the actual unemployment rate is nearly 12% as of the writing of this book.

The number of people living below the poverty line and on food stamps has risen sharply since 2009.

Many Americans fear a total collapse of the country, leading to civil war-like conditions. Those who can afford it are stocking up on weapons and food. Abortions, homosexual marriage, crime rate, overcrowded prisons, drug abuse and drug-related deaths, natural disasters, the economy, and a host of problems have plagued the U.S. in recent years.

The Super Wealthy

I recently read a report that the super wealthy are those who govern the world, for it is believed they have great influence and power over our elected officials. Super-rich people have so much money, they could settle the current U.S. national debt in cash, and they would still have a total of 31 trillion (31,000,000,000,000) dollars on hand.

Many funds of the super-rich, the report says, are in "offshore" accounts in the Cayman Islands in the Caribbean and in Switzerland in excess of $13 trillion dollars as of 2012 (The Guardian, 2012). If these huge funds were taxable, it would cover a large part of the current national debt.

A study of more than 40,000 international companies has shown that the world's economy is dominated by a small core group of huge banks and huge corporations (Tencer, 2011). This group of the super-rich consists of 147 closely intertwined companies as a "network of global corporate control" (Vitali, et al, 2011). Among them:

1. Barclays PLC   2. Capital Group Companies, Inc.   3. FMR Corporation 4. AXA   5. State Street Corporation   6. JP Morgan Chase & Co.   7. Legal & General Group PLC   8. Vanguard Group, Inc.   9. UBS Group AG   10. Merrill Lynch & Co., Inc.   11. Wellington management Co., LLP   12. German Bank AG   13. Franklin Resources, Inc.   14. Credit Suisse Group 15. Walton Enterprises, LLC   16. Bank of New York Mellon Corp. 17. Natixis   18. Goldman Sachs Group, Inc.   19. T. Rowe Price Group, Inc. 20. Legg Mason   21. Morgan Stanley   22. Mitsubishi UFJ Financial Group, Inc. 23. Northern Trust Corporation   24. Societe Generale   25. Bank of America Corporation

Powerful people wield great influence in politics, for they own the major newspapers and television stations. Americans spend over 1,200 hours a year watching TV, including Netflix and similar channels (Television Watching Statistics, 2016) and nearly five hours per day watching TV on average (Kalogeropoulos, 2015). We hear only the news that the rich and powerful want us to hear. Of course one hears good reports about the

130

President when favored by the super-rich and his party. Use of the media is an easy way to deliberately deceive the people and to convince the people to vote as the media suggests.

Since they already have most of the money in the world, is wealth enough for them? No, many of the wealthy also seek power - to rule the world financially and then to dominate all human beings as so-called credit-slaves. In such a world, we would be dependent on the super-rich and we would be expected to execute their instructions and orders.

I can't verify this is the goal of the super-rich, but the frightening report confirms my fears. According to the Bible: Satan is the god of this world, and he has only one thing in mind – to destroy, to deceive and to kill: …"hand this man over to Satan for the destruction of the flesh, so that his spirit may be saved on the day of the Lord" (1 Corinthians 5:5). And in speaking of Satan: "Now judgment is upon this world; now the ruler of this world will be cast out" (John 12:31).

Are Christians Asleep?

Some time ago, a pastor in Huntsville told me: "Jim, unfortunately, we Christians in this country don't do what we are supposed to do. We are asleep." I suppose he's right. Perhaps the same is true for Christians in Europe.

Here are the facts:

The U.S. loses 2000 churches a year. Official statistics estimate there are 154 million non-believers. The United

131

States became the world's mission field #4. Send us Missionaries!

One of the Ten Commandments is: "Thou shalt not commit adultery." But among Christians in the country every other marriage ends in divorce. The many churches in the country are almost full every Sunday; but many churchgoers are just nominal Christians without a living relationship with God. There is a movement in some churches with 40,000 attendees per service. It is something positive, but is it real?

Many mega-churches preach prosperity gospel. If you attend a service, they only preach half the truth. The sermon is mainly what everybody wants to hear: How much God loves us, and that He lets us succeed. Our success is evidence of God's love. After the service, visitors leave the church floating on cloud nine, and after a few years they realize some have indeed become very blessed and rich – the pastor and his co-pastors. I realized it over the past few years and it is both worrying and discouraging. Nevertheless, we must be bold and confident as Christians. Those who do not know Jesus, and who have no personal relationship with God are greatly disadvantaged.

- With God the Father, Jesus and the Holy Spirit, we can discuss and talk about everything, we can express our concerns and needs, and we can be sure that He will never let us down.

- Eternal life in heaven with God is already given to us through Jesus.

- He who has not Jesus, has only himself. We can give the load of each day to Jesus and He carries it for us. He who does not have Jesus, is alone to carry the load.

- We have our free life insurance, which promises us eternal joy; if you do not know Jesus, you have probably a life insurance policy, in which you constantly pay a lot of money - and when you die, you are separated forever from God and have to spend Eternity in hell. If all goes well, the spouse receives half a million.

What is God's solution for this country and its people?

The problems in this country as outlined herein, have kept me very busy and concerned. I have prayed a lot. My prayer is: "Lord, there *must* be something done about it, we cannot leave the problems as they are!" God answered me: "These problems are so large and diverse, because I withdrew Myself. My protection in the country is also being withdrawn as you can see with the attacks on 9/11/2001, the stock market crash in 2008 and the subsequent housing crisis. Satan has taken more and more ground and blinded the people. They no longer know what they are doing and what danger they really are in. Therefore, you cannot do anything about it. But I, the Lord your God, can do everything. Therefore, pray for this country and I will move My mighty arm and bring change for the better and bring revival. "

Instantly I knew: This is the solution! The change must take place in the human heart, and only God can cause that change. Once Jesus moves into a human being, he will change slowly but surely for the better. Satan leaves and Jesus reigns. The blindness leaves and people see the truth again. I imagined how such a change would affect people in politics, in the food sector, in the financial market, in all economic sectors.

Those responsible would simply no longer have the heart to deliberately produce harmful foods. The politicians would adopt laws protecting the consumer, and the manufacturers producing harmful substances would be punished.

Moreover, the politicians would do everything possible to reduce the huge debt and not create any new debts. They would decide and act for the people of their country, not for the money. They would have to pass laws to conform with God's commandments. Christians would wake up. In Congress, they would pray at the beginning of the session and ask God for advice and wisdom. School prayer would be re-established or approved. The country would evolve from negative back to positive, from cursed to blessed, and God's protection over this country would increase.

I knew that this really was God's speaking! I was euphoric. But how could I put into practice what the Lord put on my heart? This was true not only for Huntsville or Alabama, but for the entire United States, for Europe, for the whole world!

I had the thought to talk to pastors about having multi-denominational prayer sessions. So, I set up appointments with pastors of the larger churches in Huntsville and all conversations were very satisfactory, every pastor was interested. The Result: Nil. No one stepped forward to organize such an event. My euphoria was sobering and then changed into disappointment.

Nevertheless, I am still convinced that this is the only true way to get from minus to plus: Only God can save this sinking ship! In order to show our good will, my wife and I started with regular prayer meetings in which we pray for revival in this country. We have prayed now for several years. Unfortunately, no one has joined us.

Another question was posed to me: In the last book of the Bible, "Revelation of John," I read that Jesus will return at the end of time to take all of his people to Heaven - and also to judge all people. "The revelation from Jesus Christ, which God gave him to show his servants what must soon take place. He made it known by sending his angel to his servant John, who testifies to everything he saw – that is, the word of God and the testimony of Jesus Christ. Blessed is the one who reads aloud the words of this prophecy, and blessed are those who hear it and take to heart what is written in it, because the time is near" (Revelation 1-3). If I understand the Bible correctly, we are in the end times. God's Word tells us how we can see that we are in the end times:

"But realize this, that in the last days difficult times will come. For men will be lovers of self, lovers of money, boastful, arrogant, revilers, disobedient to parents, ungrateful, unholy, unloving, irreconcilable, malicious gossips, without self-control, brutal, haters of good, treacherous, reckless, conceited, lovers of pleasure rather than lovers of God, holding to a form of godliness, although they have denied its power; Avoid such men as these." (2 Timothy 3:1-5)

"You will be hearing of wars and rumors of wars. See that you are not frightened, for *those things* must take place, but *that* is not yet the end. For nation will rise against nation, and kingdom against kingdom, and in various places there will be famines and earthquakes. But all these things are *merely* the beginning of birth pangs. Then they will deliver you to tribulation, and will kill you, and you will be hated by all nations because of My name. At that time many will fall away and will betray one another and hate one another. Many false prophets will arise and will mislead many. Because lawlessness is increased, most people's love will grow cold." (Matthew 24:6-12)

There is strong evidence that Jesus is coming soon. But what does that mean, "soon"? Measured by the Word of God, it could be tomorrow or in a hundred years, God only knows. I wondered: if Jesus is coming soon, then everything will end soon, then why all this effort, if it doesn't help anyway. Yet I still keep praying every day, "Lord, not my will, but thy will shall be done!" He really knows what will happen, when, and how.

And because He has put it into my heart, I see it now as the will of God and His mission for me that I tell as many people as possible: Now is the most important time to get right with God.

He makes it so easy; Jesus paid the price at the cross for everyone. We only need to believe in Him, accept Him, thank Him and ask Him into our lives. I think before He comes again, the Lord will once again pour out His powerful grace and give many people the chance to opt for Him and life for eternity with Him. That's what I believe.

Sometime during the year after my accident, I got the idea to write this book. My son, Gilbert and my wife,

136

Silvia had told me to write some time before, but at the time they suggested it, I was not ready. Me as a writer --- that would be quite something new! Suddenly, an inner "Okay" was inside me, and I began to write.

If a book was really God's plan for me, then He will also ensure that the book is placed into the hands of those whom He chooses to read it. I pray and ask the Lord with all my heart that this book is read by many people, and that they find a living relationship with God. I also ask God that those who read this book will begin to pray regularly for revival, and to a spiritual awakening in the United States, in Germany, in Europe and around the world.

Who is going to help against evil? Jesus! He is the winner! He conquered sin, death, and the devil when He suffered on the cross and through His resurrection. What helps against darkness? Light! The darkness is powerless against the light and darkness most go away. This also applies to the darkness in this country and around the world.

Who is the light of day? Jesus! He is the only solution: Jesus is the victor over evil, and the light dispels the darkness.

When my eyes were opened for the state of the world (and I have only mentioned a few aspects), I thought: "No! We cannot accept the world as it is! We Christians must stand up and change it." But Jesus showed me that forcing change does not really help. We would only raise a lot of dust, toil and incite controversy.

When we pray to God, raise our voices to Him, and beg Him to change the world, then comes the light and evil must give way. Therefore, it is through us that God presents Himself, and not to the people who do not know what they are doing. If all Christians would come to God in prayer, He would change the people and then the world.

If Jesus with His peace comes into a person's heart, then that person knows in his heart as soon as he has done something wrong. A person won't accept his own wrong-doing, and with the help of the Holy Spirit will systematically change, little by little, to do better.

In the construction business, for example, I learned to "not take everything so precisely." After our spiritual conversion to Jesus, we were going a straight, clean way with a lot of love, in dealing with our employees, with our suppliers, and our customers.

"Treat your fellow man as you want to be treated by him" – was my new guide, in business and at home. Until I learned this, I often treated my wife as my property and as a utilitarian object, and now I treat her with respect. Our family life changed from strife and fighting, to a peaceful sharing of our lives together.

Jesus can change not just a family but also a country "from the bottom up", from the "inside out" and "from the top down". The darkness will recede. At present, the world looks so dark to me; but our Lord is ready and waiting for us to pray, pray, and pray that He may show His power.

A French priest once said: "God loves it when you bother him." (Vianney, 1786-1859)

Jesus himself has promised: "Again, truly I tell you that if

138

two of you on earth agree about anything they ask for, it will be done for them by My Father in heaven. (Matthew 18:19)

Do we want our neighbors, our boss, our city, our government and our country to change for the good? Then let us pray instead of whining. Let us confess that Jesus is Lord and that He has the solution. The solution *is* to pray, as he has taught us:

"Your kingdom come, your will be done, on earth as it is in heaven. (Matthew 6:10)

Dare to ask God for His will to be done, (instead of what you want), for He knows exactly what and when, how and where to do and go for it.

Jesus also prayed thus:

"Then he went away a second time and prayed, "My Father, if it is not possible for this cup to be taken away unless I drink it, may your will be done." (Matthew 26:42)

We can rely on it: God's plan is unsurpassably good. He has the best plan, and is much better than anything we could ever imagine. If we want to change things for the better, let us concentrate on Jesus, for without Jesus, we can do no good.

So let's confess:

• Jesus is the Lord of all, He has all the power and He can change everything for the better.

• We seek first that God's rule comes into play.

• Lord, not my will, but thy will, shall be done.

Then we should continuously pray that the Lord saves people and changes them. We will then be ready to go out and do what God called us to do. The Bible says: "If my people, who are called by my name, will humble themselves and pray and seek my face and turn from their wicked ways, then I will hear from heaven, and I will forgive their sin and will heal their land. (2 Chronicles 7:14).

17 The Most Successful People in the World

What is success?

In the media, someone is called successful if they frequently win in a sport and is also financially better off. An actor is successful when millions of fans want to see their films. A musician is successful when millions listen to their music. A businessman is successful when their company generates profit.

The following are the brief profiles of some "successful" people from sports, film and business:

Franz Beckenbauer

Soccer Player with the national team world champion and European champion. In the clubs Bayern Munich, Hamburger SV, Cosmos New York eight times champion, four times European champion, four times German Cup winner.

Franz Beckenbauer is married to his third wife. From the first marriage, there are two children and a child from a previous relationship, another child from a relationship, and from his current marriage there are two children.

The assets of Franz Beckenbauer are estimated at 150 million euros. His appearance is always friendly and pleasant, and he is healthy.

Although there are a lot of ups and downs in his private

life, the media would still describe him as very successful, particularly in view of his stately assets.

Michael Schumacher

Formula 1 racecar driver and a seven-time world champion racer (1994, 1995, 2000, 2001, 2002, 2003, 2004). Until today, he is the most successful Formula 1 driver of all time. His record: in 2000-2004 he won five world titles in a row and a total of 91 Grand Prix victories.

His fortune is estimated at over 600 million U.S. dollars. He has been married for twenty years and has two children.

After a tragic skiing accident - "a hundred to zero in one second" - he struggled for months with death and has still not recovered as of 2017.

Steve Jobs

Founder and CEO of Apple, the largest and most successful computer company in the world. His fortune was estimated at 5.5 billion U.S. dollars. He died in 2011 from cancer.

Bill Gates

Founder of Microsoft, he is one of the richest people in the world; his fortune is estimated at 72 billion U.S. dollars. He donates a large part of his assets in his foundation to help people.

Mark Zuckerberg

Founder of Facebook; his fortune is estimated at 19.2 billion U.S. dollars. He also donates large amounts of money to help many people in need.

Michael Douglas

One of the most famous movie actors with a fortune of 188 million dollars.

Michael Jackson

One of the most famous and successful musicians of all time. He left behind 400 million dollars and died due to complications with drugs.

And what does the Bible say?

All of these celebrities are well known as successful people, though their personal lives very often indicate otherwise. What do we find in the Bible? Who can be called "successful" from a biblical perspective?

Every person who is born has eternal life - the only question is where will everyone spend eternity? There is either eternal life with God in Heaven or with the devil in Hell. In Heaven there are no concerns, nor hardships, disease, pain or injury, but only joy, peace, freedom, glory, beauty and so on. In Hell, there is only pain, evil, unrest, and no beauty, nor joy, only sadness and regret.

We choose for ourselves the course we will take. While we live on this Earth, if we do not decide to follow God, we automatically go to Hell, not just for one day or a month or a year or a hundred years, but forever! The short time in which anyone can enjoy their wealth on Earth is measured as nothing in Eternity.

That is, if they did not invite Jesus into their lives and accept what He did on the cross for them, even the celebrities that I have mentioned will spend Eternity with the devil. Not even $72 billion will change the fact, because no one can buy access to Heaven. Access to Heaven is only possible with the currency that Jesus paid on the cross!

Right with God

If you do not know for certain where you will spend Eternity, I encourage you to clarify this issue now. In my case, the Lord brought me repeatedly "from one hundred to zero", and after the last accident, I knew for sure that I would spend Eternity with God. For this certainty, I am so grateful!

I wish you well, so I will ask you again to make God the boss of your life. Ask Jesus into your life. No one knows what will happen in the next second, and then it could be too late. But anyone can have the certainty that he will be with God in one second if the case arises "from one hundred to zero".

The most successful people on this earth for me are those who are right with God, who accepted His grace for themselves, and know that they will spend Eternity with Him in His glory.

How does one make peace with God? The Bible says there is only one way to our Heavenly Father and the way is through Jesus. If you want Eternal life with Him, pray the following:

Dear Lord Jesus, I believe You are the Son of God. You died on the cross for my sins and were raised on the third day. Forgive my sin and guilt. Help me to forgive those who have hurt me.

I now discard my old sinful life. Make me brand new. Strengthen my faith, give me a new spirit and a new heart. Give me Eternal life and lead me through Your Holy Spirit into all truth.

In You I will trust from this moment forward, and I want to live according to Your Word. You are my Lord and I belong to You. Amen!

Those who have given their lives to Jesus have peace with God. One can find peace with Him, for God is on their side and filling them with all the good that he has in Himself - with love and wisdom, with joy and strength. And when His followers leave this Earth, they will be in Eternity with God!

Therefore, such people are the most successful people of the world.

* * *

Epilogue

Emails from my wife after my accident

September 29, 2012

Hello,

Jim had a motorcycle accident this morning. He has several broken ribs, a punctured lung, his pelvis right is broken and they found a small blood clot in his head in the CAT scan. He has 100% memory loss.

At the moment, he is in the Huntsville Hospital in intensive care because they want to watch him. He responds to us and can move.

Thank God he did not speed because it was wet on the road - the moisture, however, caused the accident, because the bike slipped at the curve.

We are all still pretty shocked - especially Patrick, as he drove behind Jim and saw exactly how it happened.

I would ask all of you to include him in your prayers, so that everything heals quickly, and no surgery is necessary.

I will keep you up-to-date.

Thank you,

Sylvia

* * *

October 1, 2012

Thanks to all of you for your prayers and feedback. I know that Jim is going to be fine, we just have to be patient and let God do his job.

Jim was awake in our present visit - even if he does not remember anything and asks us the same questions again and again. This morning they did another CAT scan and no changes were found, which means that nothing has deteriorated.

He needs to improve his breathing, so his lung muscles are strengthened and they can remove the hose (the right lung had collapsed). He is still in the trauma intensive care unit and must remain there until his breathing has stabilized.

Thanks again for your prayers, and I will continue to keep you posted.

* * *

October 2, 2012

Jim has made some progress today. The tube was removed from the lungs and he can drink and eat.

They have taken one more x-ray of the lungs and found some liquid that should be regenerated by breathing exercises, coughing and some oxygen again. Unfortunately, he is not doing well with the exercises.

His memory is getting better from hour to hour - but this unfortunately means that we (Kevin, I and the nurse) have to be very forceful with him to get him to stay because he tries to leave the hospital. He wants to go home. A good sign, but he does not understand that he has to stay in hospital at the moment, until all is in order and he especially knows how to move with the broken hip.

He tried to negotiate with the nurse and told her that he

didn't agree to this whole thing, and once at home, he will sleep on it and then come to a decision. As hard as this is for us, the more it gives us the confidence that his memory is recovering and hopefully his short-term memory will also soon be available.

* * *

October 3, 2012

Thank you today for the many lovely wishes, and for your prayers. We vary here repeatedly from high to low, sometimes to very low - because we do not understand why all this happened.

Jim is well under the circumstances. He's still in ICU, but we hope that he can be transferred to a regular room tomorrow.

Since yesterday he gets regular food, so no more tube feedings. He no longer has to stay in bed, and is allowed to sit for a while in a chair. Today he walked up and down the corridor once with the walker (said his nurse). His breathing has improved and he no longer receives additional oxygen.

His short-term memory is still not as it should be, and all the memories are pretty messed up. Somehow, we have the impression that the things we say to him are sticking with him a little longer, and we realize that he is trying to classify everything and to remember. He also asks every time how everything is going in the company, since Werner and Monika are not there.

Yesterday the deacon from our church came and brought him communion. I still do not know how they got the news that Jim is in the hospital - but the deacon knew it and came immediately.

Tonight, when Kevin and I prayed with Jim for a good rest and quiet night, for the first time Jim also prayed - which is a good sign towards recovery.

Please continue to keep him in your prayers. Pray especially for Jim, that his thoughts and memories get better and we can bring him home soon.

* * *

October 4, 2012

Jim was transferred this morning from intensive care to a regular room. We have to stay with him around the clock, since his short-term memory has still not normalized. We believe the regular room is easier for him to recover, especially since we are always there for him.

Thank you for your continued prayers.

* * *

October 5, 2012

Jim moved yesterday to a regular room. We have the impression that his short-term memory is improving little by little because his comments are following the right order.

Unfortunately, this morning they had to insert a hose into his right lung because his breathing is too shallow. Every half hour he must do his breathing exercises, so that the lung capacity improves. Although he would rather be at home, it seems acceptable to him to be at the hospital because one of us is always with him.

Thank you again for your prayers. I hope I can bring more good news over the weekend.

* * *

October 7, 2012

Today, we are grateful for the progress made in Jim's healing process. I am also grateful for my boys, daughters and grandchildren who lovingly take care of their dad and grandpa. For me, it's nice that they play cards with Jim and train his memory, or even just sit at his bedside when he sleeps.

Of course, we realize that his thoughts and conversations are confused when he is tired, but we are certain that he continues to make progress. The many prayers that have been said for his recovery will not remain unanswered. Short-term memory has to continue to improve, and we noted that the discussions, visits are being remembered longer.

At the moment, the hose in his right side causes the most problems. I do not know whether it is the hose, the injured lungs, the broken ribs or something else that causes him pain. The fact is that he is in pain, and he cannot take a really deep breath - which of course is not good for the healing of the lung. He needs to continue to make his breathing exercises and inhale deeply every four hours.

Thanks again for all the lovely emails, for the encouragement, and the prayers - it's nice to know that so many people think of him.

* * *

October 9, 2012

This morning the tube from the lung has been removed. His breathing capacity has improved, but it still needs to be a lot better.

The best news is that he can probably go home tomorrow. He doesn't have to go into the rehab facility as the doctor mentioned in the beginning, but can do the therapies from home. We will know the details tomorrow morning.

We hope that even short-term memory will regenerate in the home environment. Thank you for your prayers and continue emails.

* * *

October 10, 2012

Jim came home around noon today!!! We hope that this positive change will allow his short-term memory to improve also.

This morning, he learned to climb stairs in the hospital (since his right leg is not allowed much strain after the pelvic fracture). So we didn't have to put a bedroom in the living room as originally planned.

Of course, everything was a little messed up for him today, but I think with a more normal flow all other things will normalize. We spent two hours in front of our front door and enjoyed the wonderful weather and sunshine. Fresh air is a real treat after all the hospital air.

Kevin talked to his teachers in college and they made it possible for him to take a class at a different time and take another course at home. This way, he doesn't have to be at college every day, and we can alternate with each other because we can't leave Jim alone at home. I can also take care of my job. What would I do if I didn't have such understanding employers and colleagues! (Thanks to Werner, Monika and the family!)

Thank you today for all the prayers and all the encouragement. It's nice to know that the distance doesn't separate our thoughts and caring.

* * *

October 11, 2012

Thank you for your continued prayers, messages, and emails. Jim is doing well so far. At least he doesn't complain about pain - except that his back hurts every now and then – but he doesn't want any painkillers.

Tomorrow morning we have the first appointment with his speech therapist, to take care of the memory problems.

Jim would like to go back to work as fast as possible - but I convinced him to wait until the next day, and to get some rest over the weekend and to wait for the appointment with the speech therapist. We hope and pray that the rest of his short-term memory improves especially through familiar surroundings at home.

* * *

October 14, 2012

Jim is well under the circumstances. The biggest problem is his back at the moment: He cannot turn to the side, and always has to lie on his back, which causes him pain.

We had a meeting on Thursday with a speech therapist who will help improve his memory.

Otherwise, he is with his walker and our dog Yellow outside and even walks a few feet without the walker. I think that even short-term memory has improved and he can remember things a little longer.

He wants to start working again on Monday. We will see how it develops. Maybe it's good if he can pursue his usual routine for a few hours. His memory could be positively affected. We will see.

I thank you all for your prayers - it is good to know that so many people think of him.

* * *

October 21, 2012

I just realized it has already been a week since I wrote to you last. Thanks for all the loving questions. Please excuse me for not answering each individually, but I just didn't have time.

Jim didn't go back to the office last week- we talked last Sunday about everything and he realized that it might be too early. At the moment, however, he is planning to start back tomorrow. Kevin and Patrick mounted a railing at the office yesterday afternoon, so that Jim can handle the stairs to his office with no problems.

In the past week he had two appointments with the speech therapist and she says that she sees progress. Also, because of the broken pelvis, he had an appointment with the orthopedic surgeon, and it went well. She is pleased with how he is

152

healing, but cautioned him to avoid putting any weight on the right leg for two or three weeks and said he must use his walker. They will begin the therapy in two or three weeks.

She has allowed Jim, however, to go to the gym to strengthen his back muscles. On Friday, he was with Kevin. The back and broken ribs cause him further problems - especially at night. He sleeps sitting partially in the chair because he has less pain.

On Monday, we also made an appointment with the doctor for his lung and ribs and then we will see how things develop. Tuesday and Thursday, we have other appointments with the speech therapist.

We are grateful to everybody that Jim is doing well so quickly - although it is certainly still a long way to complete recovery. We hope and pray that things continue to improve.

Thanks again for your prayers, emails and greetings; it is good to know that you all think of us.

* * *

October 31, 2012

Jim is since last week Monday back in the office. He has a part of his current duties - especially the planning / layout of the construction and fabrication. I try to slow him down and help, so that he does not do too much - not always with success.

Over lunch, we go home and he lies down every day to rest a little. At night, when we get home, he's pretty exhausted and is looking forward to rest and his bed.

The nights are still uneasy - he still has pain and is moving from the bed to the couch, and not just once. The speech therapist is satisfied with his progress and so is the doctor for the lung / ribs. He has confirmed that his patients prefer to sleep sitting up because it keeps the pain down.

Next week we have another appointment because of the fractured pelvis and hope he can soon put his walker away (he does it repeatedly anyway).

All in all, Jim is well under the circumstances. Also, the memory continues to improve. It will certainly take some time until everything is the same again, but we are grateful that his recovery has progressed so well.

Thanks also for your continues prayers, emails, letters, messages - they carry us forward.

* * *

November 24,2012

It is some time since my last email. Thank you for your prayers. Jim is doing okay under the circumstances. The doctor for the hip has prescribed therapy three times a week. He can also start jogging since he does not need the walker anymore. He limps a little, but that will hopefully come back all right.

The office work is still stressful for him and he is happy if he has peace and quiet time on the couch.

The nights are still interrupted by moving from the bed to the couch and back (in 1- to 2-hour intervals).

Memory: He cannot remember anything from the time in the hospital and the first two or three weeks at home. In addition, we note that, for example, he cannot recall the films that he has seen. But his short-term memory has definitely improved.

Jim wanted to see the accident scene, especially since Patrick told him the other day that the tree against which he fell was rotten and hollow. So we went last weekend with Kevin and Patrick, Jay and the kids to the accident site. I do not know how the whole thing would have been, if the tree had not been there, or if it had been a solid tree...

Thanks again for your prayers and questions, it is good to know that you think of us. For me, so many miracles have already happened. When I think about how it was on September 29, and what all has been done in this relatively short time since then...

* * *

December 21, 2012

It is again a month since my last e-mail and I just wanted to give you the latest update. I have found that I have not yet reported on Jim's shoulder. The right arm was slightly swollen after the accident, scratched and naturally green and blue. In time, Jim complained that he cannot fully move his arm, and was taken up to movement therapy.

The treatment for the hip has been addressed, but the arm hasn't improved. The doctor has asked the insurance company for an MRI because they could see no break on the X-rays, and last week Friday he had an MRI (he had to wait longer for an appointment).

Today, the doctor has given us notice that he has a rotator cuff tear. We now have an appointment on December 31st with a specialist, and then we will see how to proceed (possibly operate?).

Please keep Jim in your prayers.

* * *

February 7, 2013

Once again, I am writing to you with a request for prayers.

Jim's doctor proposed a specific treatment, and then decided how to proceed. The therapy has also so far worked, and the doctor said Jim would have to make the decision whether or not to operate in the follow up appointment.

Although the range of motion of the shoulder does not correspond to the healthy shoulder by far, Jim wanted to wait and see, because otherwise he had no problems. However, after he was no longer in therapy and was doing his own exercises, the shoulder got worse (even painful). He has now decided to perform the surgery; and the appointment is on Tuesday, 12 February.

In addition, we both have applied for a leave of absence from the company for two months. We think that we need this time off to rest. The last four months have sapped our strength and we feel exhausted, both physically and mentally.

I thank you in advance that you will continue to include us in your prayers.

Greetings from Huntsville

Sylvia

* * *

Summer 2015

For several weeks I have been working again in my brother's company, namely in the field. This was made possible by the "Green Card", which we were able to acquire in 2014 as a parent of an American citizen; so it also clarified our residency status.

Every day I visit architects, developers and designers, and offer them the services of our tile company. Some know me from before, and sometimes if the Lord guides it, we often speak about my accident, and that's when I can point to Jesus.

Everybody who hears about the accident is interested, and everyone listens when I tell them of my experience. When I mention my brain injury and that every other person does not survive, we're on the subject - I know: If I had to die, then I'd be in Heaven with Jesus and God the Father. But the Lord saved me, and therefore it is my great desire, if possible, to tell every man on this earth, that they should clarify where they goes after this life.

No one knows when the last second kicks in, nor when the final "From one hundred to zero" occurs; but the question of "Where" one spends eternity each person must clarify, as long as one lives. Whoever does not have Jesus, will spend Eternity in Hell, and I do not wish that -- even for my worst enemy. Jesus alone is the gateway to Heaven, and this gate is open to everyone!

Did my biography interest you? Perhaps you have any questions, or you want to report what you experienced while reading?

I look forward to hearing from you!

jimjstark@hotmail.com

Wimmental

Here, everything began - on the right, the "Industrial area of Wimmental": the DIY store and the Stark office building (1990s)

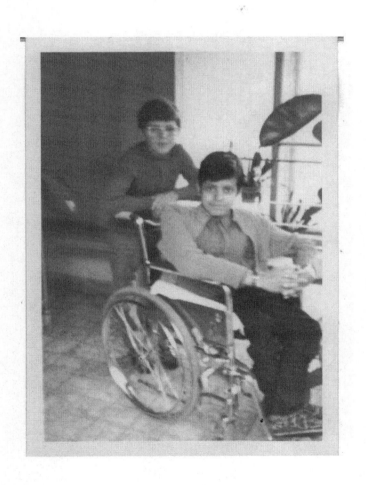

Richard and Jim
With Richard, my "angel on earth"

Wedding photo 1982
1982

160

Delitzsch
Our branch in Delitzsch gets a makeover

Screed
Nice, when the boss can help as well. At a friend's
construction site.

Truck

Our pride: the new big truck! On the right - "my" forklift (our first)

Motorcycle 1

Honeymoon – Sylvia and the Kawasaki are *behind* the camera

Motorcycle 2

My beautiful 750-Kawasaki - in memory of beautiful and difficult
weeks: Honeymoon and a severe accident shortly thereafter

Farewell

Farewell to Germany, August 2001; From left to right - Patrick, Gilbert, Sylvia and Kevin, Joachim Stark

164

Motorcycle 3

September 29, 2012: With two of my sons at the start. Half an hour later I hit the tree

Motorcycle 4

September 29, 2012: Let's go!

Accident – Road, Tree 1, Tree 2

At the scene of the accident: I had to look at it myself, and as a matter of fact; of all things, this tree was hollow!

166

Jim & Sylvia 2009

Happily married for 27 years

Family

Family reunion in Seattle, 2015

Bibliography

BankruptcyAction.com (2014). Bankruptcy Statistics for the 12-month period ended December 31, 2014. Retrieved from: http://www.bankruptcyaction.com/USbankstats.htm

Bank Trends (1998). A Time Series Model of the U.S. Personal Bankruptcy Rate. Retrieved from: https://www.fdic.gov/bank/analytical/bank/bt_9801.pdf

Breitbart.com (2013). Flashback: Obama Administration Gives $1.5 Billion To Egypt's Muslim Brotherhood. Retrieved from: http://www.breitbart.com/national-security/2013/07/01/flashback-obama-administration-gives-1-5-billion-to-egypt-s-muslim-brotherhood/

Chang, P. (2014). Brominated Vegetable Oil Dangers and Side Effects. EnergyFanatics.com. Retrieved from: http://energyfanatics.com/2014/04/07/brominated-vegetable-oil-dangers-side-effects/

Conko, G. (2007). Review of Inside the FDA: The Business and Politics behind the Drugs We Take and the Food We Eat. The Independent Review, A Journal of Political Economy. Retrieved from: http://www.independent.org/publications/tir/article.asp?a=622

Connett, P. (2010). Warning: Flouride in Drinking Water is Damaging your Bones, Brain, Kidneys, and Thyroid. Mercola. Retrieved from: http://articles.mercola.com/sites/articles/archive/2010/07/01/paul-connett-interview.aspx

Cummins, R. (2015) .Putrid Poultry. Organic Consumers. Retrieved from: https://www.organicconsumers.org/newsletter/organic-bytes-415-monsanto%E2%80%99s-%E2%80%98science%E2%80%99-doesn%E2%80%99t-add/putrid-poultry

Department of Labor Statistics (2017). Labor Force Statistics. Retrieved from: https://www.bls.gov/cps/lfcharacteristics.htm#annualstory

DiGangi, C. (2015) States with the highest foreclosure rates. Credit.com. Retrieved from: https://www.usatoday.com/story/money/personalfinance/2015/06/21/credit-dotcom-states-highest-foreclosures/71264498/

Emord, J.W. (2006). FDA Violation of the Rule of Law. Retrieved from: http://www.emord.com/Read-FDA-Violation-of-the-Rule-of-Law.html

Fortune.com (2016). 5 Things You Need to Know about the $400 Million America Sent to Iran. Retrieved from: http://fortune.com/2016/08/05/money-america-iran/

Global Cancer Facts & Figures (2012). Retrieved from: https://www.cancer.org/content/dam/cancer-org/research/cancer-facts-and-statistics/global-cancer-facts-and-figures/global-cancer-facts-and-figures-3rd-edition.pdf

Hawthorne, F. (2005) Inside the FDA: The Business and Politics behind the Drugs We Take and the Food We Eat. New York: John Wiley and Sons.

Hyatt, M. (2012). Interview: How Do You Kill 11 Million People? Why The Truth Matters More Than You Think. Retrieved from: https://michaelhyatt.com/how-do-you-kill-11-million-people.html

Hyman, M. (2011). 5 Reasons High Fructose Corn Syrup Will Kill You. Retrieved from: http://drhyman.com/blog/2011/05/13/5-reasons-high-fructose-corn-syrup-will-kill-you/

Independent (2016). Syrian refugees in Germany find country's mosques too conservative. Retrieved from: http://www.independent.co.uk/news/world/europe/germany-syrian-refugees-islam-religion-mosques-too-conservative-strict-a7384146.html

InsideGov.com (2017). Top States by Divorce Rate. Retrieved from: http://divorce-laws.insidegov.com/saved_search/States-With-Highest-Divorce-Rates

Jennifer (2016). These 12 Towns Have The Highest Divorce Rate in Alabama. Only In Your State. Retrieved from: http://www.onlyinyourstate.com/alabama/highest-divorce-rate-al/

Kaleem, J. (2012) Islam in America: Mosques See Dramatic Increase In Just Over a Decade, According to Muslim Survey. Retrieved from: http://www.huffingtonpost.com/2012/02/29/mosques-in-united-states-study_n_1307851.html

Kalogeropoulos, D. (2015). The Average American Watches This Much TV Every Day: How Do You Compare? The Motley Fool. Retrieved from: https://www.fool.com/investing/general/2015/03/15/the-average-american-watches-this-much-tv-every-da.aspx

Kim, S. (2013). 11 Food Ingredients Banned Outside the U.S. That We Eat. ABC News. Retrieved from: http://abcnews.go.com/Lifestyle/Food/11-foods-banned-us/story?id=19457237

Krejcir, R.J. (2007). Statistics and Reasons for Church Decline. ChurchLeadership.org. Retrieved from: http://www.churchleadership.org/apps/articles/default.asp?articleid=42346&columnid=4545

National Debt of the United States (2017). Retrieved from: http://www.nationaldebtclocks.org/debtclock/unitedstates

Paul, K. & Cummins, R. (2014) GMO's Are Killing the Bees, Butterflies, Birds and … Organic Consumers Association. Retrieved from: https://www.organicconsumers.org/essays/gmos-are-killing-bees-butterflies-birds-and

Paulding, J.K. (1835) A Life of Washington. (Vol.2). Retrieved from: https://books.google.com/books?id=rhgOAAAAIAAJ&pg=PA209#v=onepage&q&f=false

Reagan, Ronald (1983) President Reagan's Speech to the National Association of Evangelicals. Retrieved from: http://www.nytimes.com/1983/03/09/us/excerpts-from-president-s-speech-to-national-association-of-evangelicals.html

Reagan, Ronald (1984) Ronald Reagan's Ecumenical Prayer. Retrieved from: http://www.americanrhetoric.com/speeches/ronaldreaganecumenicalprayer.htm

Seattle Organic Restaurants (2017). What's in your meat? Drugs, cleaning chemicals, hormones antibiotics, heavy metals, toxins and bacteria! Retrieved from: http://www.seattleorganicrestaurants.com/vegan-whole-food/drugs-chemicals-hormones-antibiotics-heavy-metals-in-red-meat-fish-poultry.php

Smith, J. (2016) Monsanto, Corruption, and the Cancer Causing Dangers of GMO foods. Retrieved from: https://thetruthaboutcancer.com/dangers-gmo-foods/

Supreme Court (1962, 1963) Banning of School Prayer. Retrieved from Engel v. Vitale (1962) and Abington School District v. Schempp (1963) and Abington School District v. Schempp (1962)

Television Watching Statistics (2016). Retrieved from: http://www.statisticbrain.com/television-watching-statistics/

Tencer, D. (2011). 'Super-Entity' Of 147 Companies At Center Of World's Economy, Study Claims. The Huffington Post, Canada. Retrieved from: http://www.huffingtonpost.ca/2011/10/24/super-entity-147-global-economy-swiss-researchers_n_1028690.html

The Counter Jihad Report. The Muslim Brotherhood's "Global Project for Palestine"and "General Strategic Goal" for North America. Retrieved from: https://counterjihadreport.com/muslim-brotherhoods-plan-for-america/

The Guardian (2012). Retrieved from: https://www.theguardian.com/business/2012/jul/21/global-elite-tax-offshore-economy

UC Davis Center for Poverty Research (2016). What is the current poverty rate in the United States? Retrieved from: http://poverty.ucdavis.edu/faq/what-current-poverty-rate-united-states

Vianney, St. John (1786-1859). Jean-Baptiste-Marie
        Vianney, Third Order of Saint Francis. Retrieved
        from:
        https://en.wikipedia.org/wiki/John_Vianney

Vitali, S., Glattfelder,J.B., & Battiston, S. (2011). The
        network of global corporate control. Retrieved
        from:
        https://arxiv.org/PS_cache/arxiv/pdf/1107/1107.
        5728v2.pdf

Xu, C. (2015). *Nothing to Sneeze at: the Allergenicity of
        GMOs*. Retrieved from:
        http://sitn.hms.harvard.edu/flash/2015/allergies-
        and-gmos/

Note: Quotations of Biblical verses are from the New
International Version (NIV) of the Bible.

Made in the USA
Columbia, SC
28 March 2020